GW01418897

SPLA*M!*

Successful Property Letting
And Management

By

David Carter

SPLAM!

Successful Property Letting And Management.
ISBN: 1-4116-3444-6
© Copyright David Carter 2005. © 3D Publishing Company

Published by 3D Publishing Company, 118 Ringwood Road, Walkford, Dorset, England BH23 5RF

Please visit the web site www. dncarter.co.uk for more information on SPLAM! and other books, articles and projects.

This book
is dedicated to
Hazel Elsie Louisa Adshead

Who from 1961 to 1996
wrote me the most
inspirational letters.

I miss them still
and always will

Foreword

Welcome to SPLAM – Successful Property Letting And Management and I hope you both enjoy the read, and cull loads of useful information with regard to the interesting world of property letting and management.

Please bear in mind that facts and figures quoted can and do go out of date, housing benefit figures for example. In other words, don't take any figures as gospel; they are used for illustration purposes only. You will need to check how they stand in your area, in your time.

Neither can I be responsible for any property contracts, agreements or deals you may enter into. Only you can be responsible for that. As I say several times throughout the book, do your own thorough research and where in doubt, take professional advice.

I have taken great care in producing this guide but if you do detect any inaccuracies within the work I would be only too pleased to hear from you pointing out my mistake(s). Enjoy the read.

Chapter 1: Why a Boom?

The boom in letting property in Britain began in 1988 when assured shorthold tenancies were first introduced. This enabled landlords to let residential property for a short fixed term in the confidence they could take possession of their property at the end of the tenancy. The spectre of sitting tenants had finally been banished.

The introduction of buy-to-let mortgages shortly afterwards by six far-sighted financial houses opened the floodgates, and for the first time everyone, subject to credit checks and the ability to put up a deposit, could purchase any number of properties, purely for rental or investment purposes.

Since then the graph of property available for letting has seen a steady rise. Even with recent interest rate rises mortgage rates are still historically low. You only have to compare current rates with the John Major era to see that. The proposition of buying and renting out property remains attractive to investors, especially when compared to the paltry interest returns on cash savings offered by the banks. For many, the buy-to-let market has become known as "the pension". The property market has been, and will probably remain, the first port of call for hungry investors.

Between 1991 and 2002 I was the manager of a property management and lettings business and in that time we successfully let and sold thousands of properties across eight counties, ranging from the humblest bedsit, right up to large country houses and mansions. Famous footballers and film stars were among my clients, just as the ordinary

Joe in the street. It seems that practically everyone needs to rent a property at some point in their lives.

It makes little difference whether you are thinking of renting out a property that you or your family own, or alternatively are starting from scratch and aim to represent other landlords, this guide has been designed to help you through the minefield that can be property letting and management, and later on, development and sales too. I only wish this had been available when I started, because I know it would have saved me hundreds of pounds and countless hours of unnecessary trial and error, and sleepless nights. Whatever base you are starting from I wish you well, and every success.

The world of property can be an exciting and rewarding place. Don't let it become a headache or a millstone; there is no need for it to be so. Have fun with it; build it up at your own pace, and who knows where it might lead?

You only have the one working life, on this planet at least, so set your goals high and never lose sight of them. Promise yourself you will enjoy every minute of it, even the difficult days, (and yes there will be plenty of those too!). Retain your sense of humour, for if you can do that, you will have great fun, meet many new and interesting people, and you'll probably end up with many more friends than you began with, not to mention a great deal more money in your bank account.

Chapter 2:   Getting Started

The first thing you need to decide before you start your business, is your trading style. I'm assuming that you're not launching a PLC. That leaves you with three options.

1.   Sole Trader, e.g. J.Smith trading as Oak Properties
2.   Limited Company, e.g. Oak Properties Limited
3.   Partnership, e.g. Higgins and Harris

As in many things where a choice is available, all three have their pros and cons. If you are starting completely on your own, the sole trader option is the more likely choice for you.

SOLE TRADER:

The obvious advantage is that you are solely in charge of your own business and your own destiny. If you want to set out on a particular course or change direction you can immediately do so without consulting anyone else. The main drawback of being a sole trader, besides the fact that you do not have a second set of eyes to scan your progress, is that you do not have limited liability. Therefore if anything should go drastically wrong with your business, all your personal assets would be at risk.

You can take confidence from the fact that property management and letting is one of the least risky businesses you can become involved in. For a start you should never incur any bad debts, a major headache for most other business enterprises. But sometimes things can go wrong, the best laid plans and all that, and it is important you understand that as a sole trader everything you own is on the line, up to and including your own house. There is nothing that focuses the business person's mind more, than the possibility no matter how remote, of losing the happy home.

LIMITED LIABILITY:

The second option is to start a limited liability company. These days they can be set up for as little as £50. Buy a copy of Exchange and Mart and have a good look at the pages covering Company Registration. Ring up one or two of the registration agencies, they will send you a free information pack and you will learn a lot there if you don't already.

The advantages of trading as a limited liability company are:

- A more professional appearance
- Some protection if the business goes bust
- You may pay less tax, as you would be an employee of that company
- You involve someone else in your business

The disadvantages could be:

- You cannot own all the shares, so you have to share the benefits and profits with at least one other
- You may dissolve your controlling interest, no matter how slightly
- Some additional paperwork required, such as annual returns for Companies House

PARTNERSHIP:

The third choice is a partnership, which in the past was always the traditional way that Estate Agents operated. Remember those old fashioned estate agents trading under names such as Jones & Davies. That style of business has become more rare these days and I wouldn't go into partnership with anyone, other than perhaps my wife.

Why? Well if I had a ten pound note for every partnership I've seen over the past thirty years who have eventually fallen out, sometimes over the most trivial things, I would be a very wealthy man indeed. No matter how good a friend you may be with someone, no matter how much your thoughts and aims seem to coincide with another's, it seems that sooner or later partners do have a disagreement that often results in a messy and mucky divorce.

Just imagine spending five years with your business partner building up a successful enterprise, reaching the stage where you are managing three hundred or so properties, only to fall out over where the business was heading after that. How do you share out the clients and the properties? How do you divide the office equipment? Who keeps the office or shop premises? And indeed who keeps the trading name and the web site? Disputes of that kind inevitably end in the hands of the lawyers. And who's the winner? They are!

Partnerships also have unusual and peculiar tax rules so you'd need to discuss that with your accountant before you set out on that route. There is your first business decision. Sole trader, limited company, or partnership? What is it to be?

PREMISES:

Your next decision revolves around the premises you intend to use. Again there are three choices, always assuming you don't have suitable premises already. They are:

1. Trade from home
2. Rent an office
3. Rent a shop

TRADING FROM HOME:

Is a realistic possibility, to start with at least, and the advantages are obvious, particularly:

1. Low overheads, no rental costs
2. No travelling to work
3. Other members of the family could answer the phone while you are out

And on the downside?

1. Some clients may perceive it as a lack of professionalism
2. The phone might ring late at night
3. Visitors will seek you out, and at the most unlikely times

The advantages speak for themselves and many growing property groups such as Martin & Co, Belvoir, and Link-Up all offer start from home packages, and they do that because it works.

As for the disadvantages the phone will sometimes ring when you don't want to take calls, perhaps during your favourite TV programme, perhaps during dinner and although you may say, "I won't answer it", I'll bet you do. As for callers wandering up the path, they will seek you out wherever you may be, and of course they will often arrive at the most inopportune moment. It's sod's law isn't it?

Despite all that, it's a feasible and realistic choice, I know that for a fact, because I traded quite happily from home for nearly two years before sheer volume of business forced me to seek suitable premises elsewhere.

The moment I finally realised I would have to move out came one teatime. The good lady had prepared a particularly delicious spaghetti Bolognese and I was messily half way through the meal, stained serviette clasped around my neck, when the doorbell rang.

She looked at me as if to say, "it'll be for you, I'm not going".
I jumped up and ran down the hall almost slipping in a pile of newly laid vomit deposited there by our sick dog. I answered the door, my serviette still round my neck, as I glanced back nervously over my shoulder at the steaming mess.

A middle-aged lady and gentleman stood before me smiling. "Oak Properties? We haven't come at an inconvenient moment have we?"
"No," I stammered, dragging the red stained linen from my neck, "no, please come on in, and don't stand in that, the dog's ill".

They skirted the mess and followed me down the hall. I took them into the living room that we normally set aside for entertaining visitors; unfortunately I was half way through decorating it. The curtains were down, the furniture pushed into the corner of the room and the carpets were rolled back. It smelt musty, and it couldn't have been particularly welcoming.

Despite all that Mr. and Mrs. Ridgely became excellent clients of mine, the fact is they still are, even though I've now retired from day to day property management, other than my own. The point is, callers will, sooner or later arrive at a difficult moment. There's nothing you can do about that, other than smile and move your enterprise away from the happy home. Of course it's important you keep your own property clean and well maintained.

Potential landlords are not going to be impressed if your house needs a paint, the lawn needs mowing and there are bikes scattered around the front of the house. Naturally enough their view will be "if he can't keep his own house neat and tidy, why would he keep mine up to scratch?" And it's a fair point.

RENTING AN OFFICE:

Sooner or later it's likely that you will decide to rent an office away from your home and when you do make sure you bear these points in mind:

You Want:

1. Ample free local parking
2. Good security
3. Pleasant area
4. Room to expand
5. Reasonable rental
6. View several possibilities
7. A prestigious postal address
8. Easy to find

These may all seem incredibly obvious but when you are running around desperate and eager to set up a new business or settle into new enlarged premises it is easy to overlook the most obvious things.

Be particularly wary of:

1.   Long term leases
2.   Full repairing and insuring leases
3.   Sharing offices with unknown people
4.   Service and supplementary charges

Adequate free parking is an essential requirement. You cannot be working satisfactorily if you are forever glancing through the window on traffic warden alert. Good security too is a must; if the office is accessed through one flimsy door you can expect to arrive one morning to see it kicked in and your best new computer containing all your precious files will have vanished.

A pleasant area is not too much to ask, remember if it's a rough area and you don't feel comfortable there, not only is your office security at risk, but if you feel unhappy arriving for work, how do you think your potential clients will feel? And how will you feel on a dark unlit January night as you return to the car with a bag full of cash rent money? If you harbour any doubts about the location, find somewhere else.

Renting the right square footage is also very important, it shouldn't be too large, because you would be paying rent and rates on empty rooms, but almost more importantly it must not be too small. If you sign a long lease on a single room, and your business expands quicker than you expected, you are faced with another upheaval resulting in wasted time and expense. Don't forget you'll still have to pay the rent on that single room too, whether you are using it or not.

Some offices are reasonably priced, while others are ridiculous. You will get a better feel for the commercial market in your area, the more property you view. Choose a good postal address if you can. I eventually found two almost identical offices at similar prices. One was located at 400 Imperial Buildings, the other at Back Lane, 2a Station Approach. Some difference!

Lastly it should be reasonably easy to find. Remember that some tenants will come to the office to pay their rent and if they can't find the office, that £500 burning a hole in their pocket could find its way into the local supermarket's till. Tenants don't need much of an excuse to turn tail and hurry home. Don't give them an easy one to do so.

Always be wary of signing a long-term lease. It may look a good deal to lock in the rental figure for seven years, but can you really say with any degree of certainty how you will be doing in twelve months, never mind seven years?

When you are presented with a lease, read it thoroughly. If you're not confident to check it over yourself, pay a solicitor a hundred quid or so to do it for you. It will give you peace of mind and is well worth the money. I found an ideal office on the third and top floor of a red brick office block. The lease was a full repairing and insuring lease and that included the roof for the entire building.

The roof needed a repair, you didn't need to be an expert to see that, but worse than that, the roof needed replacing. The rental for the office was a bargain £3,500 per year. I might have signed it until a builder friend of mine pointed out that the roof repair would cost nearly £30,000 and the freeholder could have issued the necessary notices to have the repair work done at any time! At my expense. I passed on that, thank the Lord.

Neither would I share an office with someone I didn't know. I'd be too concerned they might have access out of hours? Would you be happy with a complete stranger peeking into your desk, or filing cabinet, or switching on and fiddling with your computer? No, neither would I.

Check out too if there are any service or supplementary charges. Do all of your sums carefully. Find out what the rates are, the water rates, and insurance, too, and work out precisely how much per month the office is going to cost you, and ask yourself, can you afford it? If you can, great, what are you waiting for? If you can't, walk away.

BUSINESS CENTRES:

Over the last few years Business Centres have become widespread and they do have their place. They always offer what they call "easy in – easy out" terms which are fine from the point of view that you can give a month's notice and leave, but always bear in mind, they can do the same to you, as happened to a friend of mine, two weeks after he'd spent nearly £500 on a huge new stationery package. Business Centre offices are often very small, and relatively expensive, but they do usually offer a wide range of additional services, such as telephone answering, ideal if you are trading alone and are out, or additional temporary space such as boardrooms for hire, for when you have a client you really want to impress.

But in the long run business centres are an expensive option. I wouldn't go into a business centre, but don't let me put you off, it's important that you are comfortable with whatever you decide, it's your business, you call the shots, never let anyone divert you from what you think is right. If there's a business centre in your area, go and have a look at it and see what they have to offer, then go home and do your sums, carefully.

WHY NOT TAKE A SHOP?

Shops are a whole new ball game and you need to think very carefully before taking on the responsibility of a shop. Think about these, for starters:

1. Security is a constant headache
2. Additional staff, you cannot leave a shop unattended
3. High insurance premiums, and I mean high!
4. High rentals are the norm in good areas
5. Thieving, it happens and it impinges on your thinking

I had a shop in Chester for six years and I don't think I enjoyed a decent nights sleep in all that time. In one spell the shop was broken into three nights out of four. We had sophisticated alarms, internal shutters, and expensive locks but it didn't save us.

The phone ringing at 2 or 3 or 4am on a cold winter's morning is not an experience I would wish on anyone. The voice of that bored policewoman is still fresh in my mind. "Are you the registered key holder, could you come down NOW please? Right NOW!' Lovely, not!

I wouldn't consider a shop at the outset unless I had a good supply of property and a reliable solid team of people. Yes I know the properties to let would be beautifully displayed in the window and would attract passers by and might reduce the need for so much newspaper advertising, but oh, the headaches! Shops are for people with strong nerves.

Strangers have a habit of wondering into shops often after a long session in the pub, harassing the female staff, seeking mischief and picking up almost anything that isn't nailed down. One such visitor picked up our new word processor and when asked what he was doing with it, he looked at it and said "what this?" And with that he lobbed it across the counter where it crashed onto the floor, broke into million pieces and died.

He laughed, hurried out and ran away. I chased him, for a bit, until I realised I had left the shop, and three thousand quid of rent money pretty much unattended. A shop? Not for me thanks, perhaps you are made of sterner stuff!

Chapter 3:   Getting Equipped

These days most people have computer equipment in the house. Whether the rest of the family are going to be too pleased to see it disappearing out of the front door to your new premises is another matter. Either way you will need most, if not all the following.

1   A decent computer. They are not dear these days. Just last week we bought a fantastic new system from Tesco's of all places for just £450! When I think back to the amount I spent on machines in the eighties that boasted about a hundredth of the power and cost five times as much, I shudder. I once bought an office system that cost me eighty grand, yes eighty grand! What mugs we were! A second machine is a good idea too, for backup and to do additional tasks while the first one is busy. A portable too might be useful, ideal for taking with you on calls to impress your clients. You could even do a little work in the car while you waited for your appointment!

2   A good printer of course, that system I mentioned from Tesco's had a printer included. Lasers are more likely to be black and white; ink jets can give you full colour, useful if you are printing out property details.

3   A telephone answering system, they are not dear, and one new client gained because of it will pay for the machine a hundred times over.

4   A Fax machine, despite email, fax is still used by many people.

5   A photocopier is an absolute must. There are inexpensive multi-functional machines now on the market. Photocopier, printer, and scanner all in one, but they are a little like inkjet printers in that the initial cost is small, but the running costs of cartridges can be expensive. Check out the ongoing running costs before you buy. Consider buying one of those cartridge refill kits from PC World too, and learn how to refill your cartridges. That will save you a small fortune.

6   Business stationery. With the improving quality of in house printers you can consider producing a lot of your own printed stationery, but it's still worth buying good quality two colour letterheads, if only for those all important letters to your clients. You are trying to portray an ultra professional image, and it will pay you dividends in the long run.

7   Computer software, accounting. Sage or Quickbooks seems favourite.

8   Computer software, property management, this is optional and something we'll examine in more detail later.

9   A decent and reliable car. It doesn't have to be a swish new Mercedes or Jag, in fact there is an argument that says if you arrive at a landlord's house in a fifty grand car the landlord might decide, may be even with some justification, that you are charging him too much. Whatever vehicle you use, make sure it is regularly serviced, and CLEAN! One agent I knew insisted in arriving at landlord's houses in a battered old rusty transit van. I have no positive proof it damaged his business, but I'm sure it did.

10 A digital camera. An absolute essential, especially if you want to upload photographs onto the net, a method that is becoming the norm. And they need not be expensive. I bought a super dinky digital camera in Comet for £79 and it does a fantastic job. The very first property I visited with it was a sprawling detached house in the country, the kind of property we all hanker after. The owner, a dapper man of the old school spied my tiny camera and said, "you'll never get it all in on that. The other fellow had a huge expensive camera". The "other fellow" was my rival, and the owner was instructing us both to let his house. When we saw the results on the Internet of my pictures and his, we had a heck of a laugh, for mine were infinitely superior! The owner was so impressed he rang me up and asked for the camera brand and model number.

12 A mobile phone. You may have one already. I hate the ruddy things. I hate travelling by train and listening to interminable conversations that always start in the same inane way, "I'm on the train!" As if they are on the backside of Mars! I hate the way people block up the aisles in supermarkets phoning back with the latest baked bean prices. "The Heinz are up to 49p but the own brand are down to only 15p!" They crow back, as if they are cornering the Chicago Futures Exchange, buying up the crop. The poor things don't seem to understand their call has cost them far more than the damn beans! But I do realise that in today you cannot be without a mobile phone. It will save you any number of wasted journeys; it will pay for itself many times over. A mobile phone is a must.

13   A large good diary, a page a day at least, don't
      skimp, it will become your bible.

14   Last but certainly not least, a good supportive chair!
      Don't try to save money by putting up with an
      uncomfortable chair. It's a false economy not
      buying new if you end up taking a month off sick
      through backache.

As for stationery suppliers, check out these three
companies to compare prices. Viking, Staples and Neat
Ideas. You'll find their web addresses in the trade Directory
at the end of this book.

That's it, you have all your equipment about your feet and
your premises are sorted. The next step is to set it up and
practice with it. Photograph your own house and your
relation's or friend's houses too if they'll let you! Try
uploading the pictures onto the computer. Were you
standing too close, or too far away? Were you at the right
angle, or too far to one side?

Who is that chap who keeps chanting "edgerkashun,
edgerkashun, edgerkashun"? My slogan is 'Practice,
practice, practice!' While you have the time to do so, for all
too soon you will notice you have very little spare time on
your hands. Already it's time for your next task: market
research, let's go!

Don't skimp on a good chair
Time off sick is Time wasted

Chapter 4:   Market Research

Market Research is an essential requirement. The biggest companies on the planet spend millions of pounds on market research every year and they do it because it pays dividends.

You are fortunate in that your MR will cost you almost nothing in cash terms. All it will cost is a week or so of your time, a little shoe leather and a few gallons of petrol. And don't forget, once you have carried out your initial research, to make a note in your diary to review it every six months or so. Just because Agent A is charging X on the first of January, it doesn't mean he still is come July time. It's something you need to check regularly, forever. Keep your eye on the ball. Don't neglect it.

So what precisely are you going to research? And how are you going to do it? Try these, for starters:

1. Who are your competitors?
2. What are they charging their Landlords?
3. What are they charging their Tenants?
4. Where do they advertise?
5. What additional services do they offer?
6. What local properties are available, and at what price?
7. Do they have a web site?
8. What sort of reputation do they have?
9. What are their weaknesses?
10. What are their strengths?
11. What hours are they open? And most importantly of all
12. Where can you better them?

CREATE A RESEARCH CHART:

Get yourself a large piece of paper and rule it out so you can make a chart detailing your competitors, their charges, and services and don't forget to leave a column for yourself. You can fill in your own figures once you've analysed the competition.

Perhaps you feel a little uneasy prying into the affairs of other businesses? Well don't! Why? Two reasons.

Firstly, as you become more successful they will sure as hell start taking an interest in you and your business, and what you are doing and sooner or later they will look at ways and means to undercut and undermine the new upstart. That's the way of the world, it's dog eat dog out there, it's not after you Claude! It's eat, or be eaten. That is the free market. You compete or you go out of business, and anyone who tells you differently is talking baloney. As long as it's legal and ethical, it's OK. Don't overstep the mark; you will know in your own mind what is acceptable and what is not.

The second reason is that every large business monitors its rivals all the time. Tesco's check out Sainsbury's who check out Asda's prices every day. There's nothing underhand about it, they send mystery shoppers into each other's stores to check out every goddamn thing. The prices, décor, checkout arrangements, everything. There's nothing secret about it, they admit it, and they would be neglecting their own customer's interests if they did not keep a sharp eye on what their competitors were doing.

What you are doing is precisely the same thing. You need to know what your competitors are charging, you need to know the terms and conditions they are trading under, if you don't, you will lose business and struggle to survive, nothing is more certain. Not to do so would be foolish in the extreme.

<u>WHERE TO LOOK FOR INFORMATION:</u>

There are three places where you can obtain this information.

1. The competitor's shops
2. Their Internet sites
3. By telephone

Go and have a look at all your competitor's shops. Yes you will be pestered and questioned as to what precisely it is you are looking for and you may need to be a little creative. You could say you are thinking of buying a buy-to-let property and ask what they would charge to let and manage it.

There is nothing wrong in that, you ARE thinking of buying a buy-to-let property and renting it out, even if you don't do it now, you ARE thinking about it. Ask for their terms and conditions. The chances are they will give you their full fact pack of information and details on everything they have on property letting, from lists of properties available to details of gas and electrical safety requirements. It's all market intelligence, seize it all, every last piece, take it home and read the lot of it, every last sheet. Remember, you are going to become the best-informed property agent in the county. When you have finished, no one will know more about rental property in your area, than you, that's your aim, your goal and you've just taken your first step to achieving it.

Internet sites provide a wealth of free and easily obtained information without fuss. The amount of intelligence you can glean from sites varies from one to another but keep looking and download terms, conditions and fees and any other facts and statistics that interest you. By the time you've finished you'll need a new filing cabinet to house it all, if you haven't one already.

Occasionally you'll come across an agent, a competitor remember, who doesn't have a shop or an Internet site, or their web site might be very basic, and these you will need to ring up to find out what you want to know. It's easy ringing them, tell them the same thing as before, that you are considering a buy-to-let property and could they send you details of their services.

If you are intending ultimately to trade from home it may be an idea to get them to post the details to a close relative or friend, whatever you feel comfortable with, but remember you do need to obtain that information one way or the other. You don't want to be launching your business not knowing what your main competitors are charging and what they have to offer. That would be unforgivable.

When you've gathered everything together and all the squares on your chart have been filled in, you will have a list of ALL your potential rivals and their charges. You will now also have an idea in your mind what you can charge your clients.

MAKE A PROPERTY LIST:

The next step is to collate a list of all the properties that are available in your area for rent and the rental values placed on them. Far and away the best place to glean that information is in the local press. Make an effort to obtain ALL the local publications that circulate anywhere in the area you intend covering. The freebie papers, the weekly paid papers, and the local evening paper. They usually run a property supplement one night a week, most often on Wednesday or Thursdays. Get them all, even if you don't usually buy newspapers.

And while we're talking about areas, if you are happy to drive, don't restrict yourself to too small an area without good reason. It doesn't take long to drive thirty miles, traffic permitting, so why restrict yourself to the local ten miles? Remember, you are looking to sign up business, and as long as it is not too far away, and is profitable, consider it seriously.

Start to list all the properties available in price order on your word processor/PC. It's good practice and every time you type out a property and price it will reinforce those values and areas in your mind. You don't need to know the exact address at this stage. Your list could well look something like this. Keep them in strict price order; it's easier compare prices that way.

PROPERTIES TO LET:

Barton, studio flat unf 300.00 pcm
Willsdon 1 bed fff unf   395.00 pcm
Hartley 2 bed purpose built 2nd ff unf 450.00 pcm
Barton, 2 bed furn terrce 495.00 pcm
Hartley 2 bed unf semi det hse 525.00
Barton 3 bed pf semi det 595.00 pcm
Keeley 3 bed det unf bung 695.00 pcm
Hartley 4 bed unf det hse 795.00
Bromton 4 bed fully furn det 850.00 pcm
Narkville 4 bed fully furn det s/pool 1500.00 pcm
Grandiosa 6 bed detached farmhouse 1850.00 pcm

Of course these properties are not yours, that's irrelevant, but you are already beginning to add to your expertise of the local property market. Get to learn all the shorthand; did you understand everything there? There wasn't anything too difficult. Unf, pf, ff, are obviously unfurnished, part furnished, and fully furnished. Fff is first floor flat, pcm is per calendar month, you'll soon get the hang of all the property speak, and just to make sure you do there's a list of terms and abbreviations at the end of this book.

Incidentally I've studied the pricing of rental property throughout the kingdom and in the vast majority of areas properties are priced on a calendar monthly basis. There are exceptions to this of course; London being the obvious one, where prices are invariably charged on a weekly basis and are often the same as the prices being charged in the provinces per month!

Nevertheless even in some provincial areas some landlords and agents stick up prices on a weekly basis so look out for it. It is vitally important you compare like with like.

Charging rental on a four weekly basis is very rare these days and is just downright confusing. The public see it as a way greedy landlords have of squeezing an additional rental payment from the tenant every year, and they have a point. Where rent is charged on a four-weekly basis it is probably to do with housing benefit type properties. Get it clear in your own mind; is it a weekly, four weekly or a monthly price?

CONVERTING RENTS:

There is only one way to convert accurately a weekly price into a monthly one. It's a simple calculation. Take the weekly price, say £90, multiply it by 52 (to give you a price per YEAR), and then divide the answer by 12 to give you the exact equivalent monthly figure.

Thus £90 per week becomes £4,680 per year.
Divided by 12 = £390 per calendar month.

Note: Never multiply a weekly rental figure by 4 to give a monthly figure. If you do that you will cost your client, (the landlord or yourself) 4 weeks rental in a year. To make it easier for you there's a table at the end of this book that gives you at-a-glance conversions.

If you are outside London try to run your business on a per calendar month basis, especially if that is how all or most of your competitors operate theirs. The more standardisation you can introduce, the easier things will be.

TO RECAP:

You have identified all your local competitors and have spoken to or visited each of them. You have examined their web sites and you have a good idea what they are charging their landlords and tenants. You've compiled a rough list of properties available in price order and already you are beginning to get a feel for the local rental market.

You have kept your ears open and may have heard a piece or two of interesting gossip about Williams and Sons who are opening soon in Halton, or Red Horse Rentals who are closing down. (It never ceases to amaze me that some staff members discuss the most confidential things in shops in front of the public as if parents in front of very young children. Do they really imagine we are closing our ears?).

But most important of all you have identified one or two agents who seem a little complacent, perhaps tired even. May be they are charging a little too much and doing too little for it? No doubt it will be from these agents who you will eventually take a proportion of your new business. There is no need to target specifically a particular agent. If there is an agency that doesn't cut the mustard you will annexe a slice of their business almost unknowingly.

LIASE WITH THE MEDIA:

The next task is to speak to all the local newspapers and magazines, both paid and free papers, that carry any property advertising, and ask them for their advertising rate card. Tell each of them you are just starting in business and ask them for a special introductory deal. You can be a little cheeky, mention the Herald has already offered a 33% discount on your first booking, and surely the Post could better or match that.

One thing is certain, DO NOT pay full rate card prices, remember everything is negotiable, especially advertising costs; the prices on these cards are deliberately inflated. The papers expect to accept less, and they will do so. You can also ask them to keep you informed of any last minute offers and cancellations. These can often be picked up for a fraction of the cost of full price ads. I once bought a full-page ad for just £100 when the normal rate was £960! The publisher was so desperate to fill the page, and I could do so at ten minutes notice. When you see a bargain, snap it up!

If publishers get into the habit of ringing you with attractive last minute offers do your best to take them, if you don't, someone else will, and next time you might not see the offer. On the other hand be alert to the possibility publishers will sometimes ring very excitedly with what they say is a very special deal, but look at it carefully, is it?

ALWAYS BID LESS:

They will often do this after they've had a frantic sales meeting; perhaps they've failed to meet their targets. Sometimes these offers are more bluster than real discount, and remember whatever they offer you, BID LESS! You'll be amazed how many times they'll take you on. Often they'll say "but don't tell Bloggs & Sons down the road we did it for that ridiculous rate". The truth is they are probably saying precisely the same thing to Bloggs!

Bear in mind too you always have the option to say I'll think about it and put the phone down. As the copy deadline nears and the spaces remain unsold you may get a call back accepting your lower bid. Remember, the nearer the deadline, the cheaper unsold advertising space will be. They have to fill it with something and would rather be paid LOW rate, than NO rate!

The fact is if you can get a third off the price on every ad, your fourth ad works out FREE, if you can get 50% off through shrewd negotiation, that means half of your ads will run for FREE. Newspaper Publishers are very flexible, they hate to lose a customer and they hate it even more if they suddenly see your ad in their rival's paper. They study their competitors even more closely than you do. Take advantage of the fact. Make the most of every advantage that comes your way.

When you've completed that, you have one last piece of MR to conduct before you have finished the initial burst. Take a pen and notebook and visit every newsagent and shop window notice board in the area, and indeed any other notice boards that you are aware of, in supermarkets, clubs, public notice boards, libraries, and jot down all the properties that you find to let.

On most of the notice boards you'll find at least one property and sometimes more. These properties are usually from private landlords and they do provide interesting and valuable MR. These properties are not YOUR properties, not yet anyway, but neither are they another agents, and with a little bit of effort they could become YOUR properties. Take the details home and list them in your diary and save them for another day.

Chapter 5: Your Services, Fees, & Literature

Most property letting and management agents offer two basic services. They are:

1. Find a tenant only
2. Find a tenant AND manage the property on an ongoing basis

There are many other potential income streams that can be introduced such as inventory preparation, repairs, insurance, solving landlords disputes and others too but the two listed above are the main planks of most letting agent's business and they will provide the bulk of your income.

You need to set your prices, bearing in mind, but not desperately discounting, your competitors. You do not need to discount your competitor's prices and for very good reasons.

<u>YOU ARE VATLESS!</u>

Firstly, as you have just started to trade, your turnover cannot possibly be above the £60,000 minimum turnover figure (at the time of writing) required before registration for VAT becomes compulsory. Whatever your fees are, they are VAT FREE! The chances are your competitors will be charging VAT as an extra at the foot of their bills. This gives you an instant and immediate 17.5% advantage over almost all your rivals from day one. It's an important advantage, so USE it to the full and I'll show you how to do precisely that later on. The vast majority of landlords cannot reclaim the VAT, as they are not VAT registered so

31

a VAT free agent as you will be, is a definite attraction. Some agents charge a flat fee to find a tenant only, say £275. Others may charge half of a month's rental, or the equivalent of 3 weeks rent. That's what I charged and I never experienced a problem with landlords accepting that figure. Set your fees as high as you can, as long as they remain competitive. Remember, half a month's rental on an £850 pcm property is a heck of a lot better than having a fixed fee of £275.

FIXING YOUR MANAGEMENT COMMISSION:

For ongoing management most agents charge a percentage ranging between 8% and 15% or more. I expect that 10% will be a commonly quoted rate, and if that's widely quoted by your competitors I suggest you set that rate too. Again you are VAT FREE, so you are already operating at a serious discount to your rivals. There should be no need to reduce the percentage figure as well.

On managed properties you may also be able to charge a modest fee when the property is let as well as the percentage; I always charged a flat £100 and then 10% on the entire collected rental. I cannot set your fees for you, I have no experience of your area, your markets, or your competitors, but I would strongly urge you not to charge too little. It isn't necessary. Remember, many more businesses close down because they are charging too little, rather than too much.

And another thing, if you have a particularly attractive client, and I don't mean a pretty face, I'm talking commercially here, someone who may have three or four properties to let, you can always reduce your price a little by offering a quantity discount. That's fair enough. You can always reduce your fees from your starting level, but it is very difficult to increase them if you discover you've set them too low in the first place.

PREPARE YOUR WRITTEN MATERIAL:

You've set your fees and the next task is to prepare the written material you'll want to mail to potential landlords when they contact you. These details need to be neat and tidy, and spot on. It is not necessary for you to fork out many hundreds of pounds on glossy brochures and files. It is far more important the details are neat, with clear grammar and NO spelling mistakes and the content is correct.

Learn how to spell 'accommodation' if you don't already. The easy way to remember that one is, it's double M AND double C. I am constantly amazed how many estate and letting agents cannot spell the word, and not just the small independents either. Don't believe me? Take a trawl through some of the big property web sites and you'll see what I mean.

When I first set up my landlord's details I made the mistake of trying to be all things to all people and tried to cover every possible property fact and requirement. When I'd finished my brochure resembled a telephone book with countless do's and don'ts. I listed in great detail all the things I would do for the landlords and all the tasks I would carry out.

I remember one colourful landlord when I presented him with the tome said to me, "what the hell's this? I haven't read a book in my life, and I'm not bloody well starting now!" He thrust it back at me and said, "just get on with it, it's what I pay you for!"

TOO MUCH INFORMATION CAN CAUSE PROBLEMS:

My tome wasn't necessary and in the end cost me money when a particularly vicious landlord took my company to court because one minor item on the list of duties we said we'd carry out was dealt with in a questionable manner.

Fortunately the judge saw through the guy and realised he was only out to obtain a sizeable chunk of compensation on the back of a technicality, and threw out the case, but it taught me a valuable lesson.

I abandoned the phonebook style brochure and introduced a slimmed down landlord friendly version. The landlords appreciated its clarity and we never had a problem with it again. We do, rightly or wrongly, live in an increasingly litigious society and you can expect that at some point someone will examine your brochures with the sole aim of making mischief. The more duties and tasks that you say you will carry out, the more chance there is that one day you will miss something and leave yourself open to attack. Brevity is the order of the day.

Take another look at the paperwork submitted by your rivals, especially the big nationals. Some of them, just as on their 'for sale' property particulars are becoming slimmed down to the bare bones. Their reasoning is 'if we don't include room measurements, we can't be prosecuted for getting them wrong.' There is a strong case here for less being more.

You can be assured that the big national concerns have had highly paid lawyers paw over their details time and time again and you can be confident they are legally correct. I am not saying copy their details, indeed you must not copy verbatim their stuff. But you can take inspiration from some of their work and you can incorporate many of their ideas. And when you have finished your own documentation, if you need a little extra reassurance that everything is fine and dandy, legally speaking, bite the bullet and let your solicitor glance over it. Yes it will cost you a few quid, but you will be reassured that everything is correct.

CONSIDER MANAGEMENT SOFTWARE:

Alternatively you can sign up to one of the many property software management programs that abound. These vary in price and quality immensely, but they do provide checked documentation. I will be looking again at the whole business of property orientated computer programs and documentation in a later chapter

You will also need to prepare a tenant's application form. These are fairly standard from one agency to another and should not present a problem. When you sign up to one of the referencing agencies they will provide you with a tenant's application form template if you want it. The fee the tenant pays with their application form is usually around the £100 mark.

Some agencies charge per person, while others charge per application. In other words if a single person applied for a house the fee payable would be £100, but if 4 people applied to share a house the fee charged by some agencies would be £400, and that's a big difference to the agent's profit margin. Charge what you can reasonably achieve.

Your market research guide will show you where to pitch your fees, but one word of warning; many tenants will expect a refund of their application fee if they are unsuccessful. Most large agencies do not entertain returning such fees, ever. Some of the smaller ones do. Whichever ruling you introduce, make sure that it is clearly noted on the application form that the fee is NOT refundable (if that is the case). Where this can cause strife is when you have a property that is highly sought after and you may receive a large number, say eight different applications for the same property, and correspondingly eight application fees.

In that case I would never retain more than one fee, and if you decide to do so you can expect justifiable hassle from the tenants if they suspect as much, and perhaps even a telephone call from Trading Standards officers. I don't believe there is anything illegal about retaining all eight fees, but you do not want to gain a reputation for sharp practice. You have to be comfortable with your policy on this.

One other word of warning on charging tenants fees. It is illegal for any agency to charge a potential tenant any fee just to register them on your books. If a tenant rings up and asks if you will keep a look out for a one bedroom flat in a certain area you cannot say "our fee for that would be £50". That is a definite no-no, fees can only be charged to tenants to process their application for a specific property.

ALWAYS COLLECT TENANT'S FEES UPFRONT:

Never accept an application from a tenant without them paying the fee upfront. If they say they will pay later they probably won't. They certainly won't if you don't offer them the property. Be aware also that if they have paid by personal cheque the tenant can stop that cheque at any time until the funds have cleared, and they very well might if you turn them down. A cash application fee is the best kind.

I will look again at processing tenant's application fees in a later chapter. By now you should have set your fees, for landlords and tenants, you've produced your own tenant's application forms and you've started to put together the landlords Fact Pack, its high time to progress on to seeking out those precious properties, the lifeblood of your business.

Chapter 6 : Locating Properties & Gaining Instructions

There is no doubt that gaining instructions to let property is the most challenging task facing any new agency. If you have no property to let, you have no business. You must leave no stone unturned to seek out as quickly as possible property to offer to your potential clients. It is your overriding concern; it is the only thing that now matters to you. GET PROPERTY!

Ideally you should be aiming for your very first newspaper advertising campaign to include some property that you actually have to let, and that is your target. It won't be easy, but with a little ingenuity you should be able to achieve it.

Some people starting new agencies seem to think that somewhere there is a directory, similar to a yellow pages, that lists "Landlords", and all they have to do is ring up and say "please mister landlord may I have some properties now?"

It would be fantastic if such a comprehensive directory existed, but it doesn't. There is only one way to gain instructions, and that is by hard work and effort. But it will be worth it; it's a little like getting a snowball running. When you start rolling the ball it's tiny and inconsequential, but as you slowly get it moving it suddenly starts to grow, then almost by surprise it appears quite large and the strange thing is the larger it becomes, the larger and quicker it grows.

WHO WOULD YOU USE?

Think about it this way. If you had a property to let and you glanced in the paper and saw HUGE & IMPRESSIVE HOMES Ltd advertising sixty properties to let and beneath their ad TINY HOUSES Ltd were advertising two properties, who would you approach to let yours?

The odds are that HUGE & IMPRESSIVE will pick up an additional ten to fifteen instructions that very week, while TINY will be lucky to pick up another two or three. Why? Because generally speaking people are attracted by success. It's exactly the same with estate agencies. Look in any local newspaper anywhere in the country and you will find thrusting and modern agencies, many of them recently established, let's call them MODERN & CUTE, running several pages of properties, probably in full colour.

Over the page you will find OLD & TIRED, Estate Agents, running a small ad with a few homes in black and white in a dated designed advertisement. Again, who would you choose to sell your home? Not many opt for OLD & TIRED, because people like success. They swarm to success like moths to a light, because they believe rightly or wrongly that the larger thrusting more successful agency will produce the required results. They want the success to rub off on them.

BECOME HUGE & IMPRESSIVE:

Your initial task may be to gain instructions, but your longer-term aim is to become HUGE & IMPRESSIVE yourself, and as quickly as possible. With careful planning, hard work and perseverance you will become HUGE & IMPRESSIVE almost before you realise it. Trust me on this; there is nothing to stop you.

But before then, let's look at where you are going to find those elusive first properties. Here's where they'll be found.

1. Property that you already own
2. Property you are going to buy
3. Property that your friends and family own
4. Your own house, yes the house you live in now
5. The cards you noted in the newsagents windows
6. The small ads in the local newspapers
7. By direct advertising
8. By approaching existing landlords you may know

To have purchased this book in the first place demonstrates that you have an interest in property. If that's the case perhaps you have a property to let, may be even more than one, available for rental, in which case you will include it in your first advertising. If you don't already own property, the question must be, why not? Why don't you acquire some?

Buy-to-let mortgages are available everywhere these days. You will need perhaps 15% - 20% deposit, thus on a £100,000 flat you will need to put up £15,000 to £20,000. If you can find that, you are already in a position to purchase property that can then be offered to the public.

It is possible to buy property for even less deposit than that, even no deposit at all sometimes. Check out the newbuild stuff in your area, some of them offer to pay your deposit, especially if you are a first time buyer. There are also dozens of so called "property clubs" that have sprung up offering no deposit deals, but be very wary of them. They are for the most part unregulated and before parting with money to pay their large fees, ask yourself, "What exactly am I paying for?" The discounts they seem to offer are often available to anyone prepared to research the market, for FREE.

If you haven't the necessary capital, or a bad credit record hampering you from obtaining a mortgage, your target must be to generate the cash in order that you can acquire your first rental property. Concentrate too on getting your credit record straight, just because you might have had problems in the past does not mean you can't put it right in the future. Time is a great healer when it comes to repairing credit ratings. I know what I am talking about.

THE IMPORTANCE OF YOUR OWN REGISTER:

Of course there is good money to be made in property letting and management, but don't fall into the trap of spending all your time and energy looking after other people's portfolios. Always be on the look out for ways and means of how you can start and increase YOUR OWN portfolio.

In ten years time you don't want to be sitting back in your chair congratulating yourself on how well all your clients have done, probably in a large part based on the efficient and professional service you have provided. You want to be amongst them, and well up the list as to the degree of success achieved. After all, you will be in the best position to do so.

Why? Because you'll have knowledge of the tenants before any of your landlords, you can pick and choose them, and put only A1 tenants into your own homes. In addition you'll also get to learn of some properties that come on the market as some landlords bail out and sell. Often these landlords are seeking a sharp exit and are looking for a quick sale, perhaps even at slightly below current prevailing levels. There is nothing illegal or underhand about that. If a landlord tells you they are thinking of selling, tell them you are interested, and ask them what price are you looking for? When a bargain comes along, snap it up! If you don't, the competition surely will. You can appreciate that you'll be sitting in the best seat of all when it comes to building your own portfolio. Don't let the opportunity pass you by.

The number of property agents who don't own any property constantly amazes me. When I ask them about it they almost always say the same thing, "I was just too busy to build up my own portfolio." That's ridiculous. Don't fall into that particular trap. Never be too busy to look after yourself. No one else will.

RENT OUT FRIEND'S PROPERTIES:

Think of all your friends and relatives. Do any of them have a property standing empty? Have any of them recently lost their parents? Perhaps they have a pretty detached bungalow standing unloved and unattended. Perhaps they have a property on the market for sale that is simply not moving. In any of these cases ring them up. Tell them you have established a property letting and management business called PROGRESSIVE LETS and you are looking for additional property to let.

Point out to them if they have property standing empty and not moving, that instead of it costing them money, as it would be, suggest they might consider renting it out, for say £700 a month, if only for one year. Stress the monetary aspect. "Wouldn't you rather have an extra £700 a month in your pocket?" Money talks, believe me. Paint a bright picture. "Think of the holidays you could have!"

After a year they could always replace it on the market when the sales environment might be more vigorous. If they rented it out for one year they could receive as much as £8,400, less your fees. That's not to be sneezed at, and it's sure as heck better than nothing at all plus bills while it stood empty. An empty property is a deteriorating property.

I never know why people are in such a hurry to sell their parent's homes when they are left to them anyway. You can only sell a house once, you can rent it out forever, and the rental figure should increase every year. I bought a house in Ellesmere in Shropshire in 1997 from a family whose parents had passed away. It needed decorating, but absolutely nothing else. I paid £53,000 for it. They wanted the cash. It's now worth in the region of £150,000 and it's been successfully rented out every month since. It's my pension. (One of them!)

Someone else has been paying the mortgage for me and the house has cost me nothing other than an annual gas safety check, and a new lock on the garage door. If I needed any additional cash I could go to the bank and they'd give me anything I wanted, within reason, on the back of that one deal alone. Think about it. Do you have a friend desperate to sell a property? Perhaps you should have a quiet word with them, and point out the alternatives. Quote that example if it helps.

The benefits of this deal are there for all to see. So why do so many people rush to sell inherited property so quickly? It's because they are dazzled by the thought of banking so much cash. Perhaps they need the money; they have probably never had so much ready cash before in their lives. They might never have again and they are in a rush to spend it. A round the world cruise and an expensive new German car are usually high on the agenda.

Within a few years the chances are the money will be gone. Remember you can only sell a house once, you can rent it out forever, and it will still increase in value. If you know anyone in a rush to sell an inherited house, have a quiet word with them. Point out the merits of letting. In the longer term they will thank you. In the shorter term you will have picked up another valuable instruction.

RENT OUT YOUR OWN HOUSE:

Why don't you rent out your own house? Yes, I mean the one you live in now! That's a ludicrous idea! But is it? Remember when you compiled that list of properties available in your area. Where exactly would yours have fitted in, in the price scale of things? Let's imagine you own a semi-detached house worth say £650 per month on the rental market, so what price would it take for you to move out and rent it? £750 a month, £850 a month, £950 even?

Take the £850 a month figure, imagine for a moment renting out your house for that amount. The first thing you would need to do is find somewhere else to live. But you already know you could rent a similar, possibly even a slightly better house for £650 per month, you've checked your lists. So why not move? Yes, you would have some moving costs, but you will be making a clear £200 a month profit, that's nearly two and half thousand pounds in a year, and more importantly you would have another house to let.

Perhaps you could even consider renting a slightly cheaper house for a year or two. Is your present house a bit big for you? Perhaps the children have grown up and left home. Why do you need a 3 or 4 bedroom house? You probably don't. A nice little bungalow would do fine, wouldn't it?

If you rented a small bungalow for a year or two for £450 a month and rented yours out for £850 you'd be well on your way to a £10,000 surplus over two years and well on your way to buying a second property. And don't forget you haven't sold your own house, you still own it and someone else is now paying the mortgage for you, and you can move back in as soon as the existing tenancy agreement ends, if you really want to. Who knows, you might develop a liking for that bung!

PRICE IT UP ANYWAY!

Even if you have no intention of renting out your own house, I suggest you price it up and prepare the details as if you were. If nothing else it will be good practice and you now have the very first property to place in your ads. Well done, you're very first instruction, you've INSTRUCTED YOURSELF! Not many people can say that, and don't forget to over value it. If you are going to even consider moving, it must be worthwhile. If you have a mortgage on your own property you will need to seek permission from the mortgage company before you can let it. This is almost always forthcoming, unless you have a poor payment record.

Think of everything from a commercial angle, even if you haven't been used to thinking that way before. Think pounds, think profits, think of an angle where you can make the very best from your assets. Remember it's a much more realistic route to success by taking a reasonable profit from hundreds of deals, than by making one huge killing. It's what you are aiming for. Lots of deals mean lots of profits.

And there is another benefit of over valuing. When you advertise your property for £850 a month it could attract quite a bit of interest. Some people will rightly deduce it's overpriced, but other landlords might think "blimey, if they can get that figure they must be good, perhaps they could get that kind of figure for me!"

Landlords are in business for one reason and one reason alone, to make money! They are not a charitable organisation or a Housing Association, they are in it for the cash, and they are attracted by success and high rental figures. Always have been, and always will be.

It's one of the oldest tricks in the book, to overvalue properties to gain the instruction. Almost every new estate agent in the country does it in their first month. You can do it too, but don't take on too many at high figures because the chances are you will struggle to get them away. But bear in mind your first target is to get the instructions on the book, even if they are slightly expensive. It doesn't matter. Take them. Instructions always attract further instructions. Trust me.

LANDLORDS WILL INSTRUCT YOU:

If you think you'll never persuade landlords to trust you and instruct you to let their properties, you are wrong. Why? Because some landlords are so hyperactive they cannot see a new letting agency advertising in the local papers without instructing them too. Perhaps they think they are missing something, after all they don't know anything about you. Perhaps they imagine you are the best property agent in the county and they haven't used you at all. Let them think it. It won't be long before you are.

It's just the same when it comes to houses for sale. Take a walk round any town and look in the estate agent's windows. I guarantee that you will find one house that is in just about every window. Some landlords are simply not happy unless they are on every letting agent's lists, so they will instruct you, really they will, because they want to be on your lists too. After all it doesn't cost them anything does it? No let no fee, isn't it? They'll ring, you can be sure of it. Sooner or later, they'll ring you.

SHOP WINDOW CARD ADS:

The next place to find properties is on those cards you noted in the shop windows. Dig them out, and ring them up. Introduce yourself, perhaps something like this.

"Hello this is John Williams, I've recently started a new property lettings agency, KEY LETTINGS and I noticed your property advertised in the newsagents window".

At this point the person you are speaking to may well interrupt. Why? You'd need to understand why they are trying to let via a shop window to answer that question. They are using the shop window because first it is cheap advertising, but secondly because perhaps they have previously had a bad experience using an agent. May be the agent did a runner with his rent. It happens. They might say rather curtly "Never use agents!" or words a lot worse than that. They might even slam the phone down, leaving you staring at the dead phone with a ringing in your ear.

They might use the shop window because they believe they know all about property letting and in that case what would they need an agent for? There are thousands of amateur landlords out there. Many of them have watched a few property TV programmes and think they know all about property management. They don't. Some are very clued up and efficient, but many others are exactly that, amateurish.

Did you see an edition of Tenants from Hell recently where a landlord prepared his own tenancy agreements? He'd entered the figure six next to the months/years paragraph but instead of deleting years he'd fatally deleted months. The result was he was left with a tenant who not only turned out to be a poor payer but a tenant bearing a tenancy agreement locking him in to a fixed rental for SIX years. Would a professional agency have made such an amateurish mistake? I doubt it. I hope not. I never did. Nor will you.

If the landlord on the phone says, "we don't pay agency fees", you could perhaps get round that objection by up valuing the property. After all if the landlord was seeking

£500 per month, you would only have to up value it to £550 for the landlord still to receive the figure he wants (after your 10% deduction). Impress on the landlord there is NO Let – NO Fee, so what have they to lose? And don't forget to bleat on about NO VAT and of how much attention you would be able lavish on him and his business, since you are a new, and very keen!

Some landlords will see the sense of that and will agree to meet you at the property to discuss it further. Some landlords won't have anything to do with you even if you could get £1,000 per month and provide them with free beer forever. Some landlords are like that, after all they are human beings, and all human beings are different!

Some landlords are rude, stupid, arrogant, and thick! Thankfully they are in the minority. But hey, put the phone down, it's their loss, you were offering to advertise and promote their property FREE of charge without any costs to them whatsoever, yet they still wouldn't talk to you. It's their loss! There are plenty of other fish in the sea. Put the phone down and move on to the next card.

Then there are the confused outright amateur landlords who are only too pleased to talk to someone about their properties. These kinds of contacts are rare and need to be courted vigorously. Arrange to meet them as soon as possible. Look very carefully at the value they have placed on the property. If they are complete beginners it is highly likely their figures might be wrong, perhaps way out, either too much or too little.

If you seriously think you could get an extra £50, £75 or £100 per month for their house, tell them as much, it will be brownie points in the bank for you, and remember you have no idea if this person owns another house, or another ten. If you can seal a good deal for them on this initial property you may have made a contact for life. If you offer a pleasant and efficient service that person may well tell their friends in the Conservative Club or the Bridge Club all about you. You never know where it might lead. You don't know who they might know and you have no idea what additional telephone calls you might receive thereafter.

COLD CALLING:

Cold calling is a difficult thing to do, make no mistake about it. So do it when you are feeling at your brightest. Smile as you are talking. People don't need a videophone to see someone smiling on the phone. Don't be put off by the boorish replies of know-alls. They live in every town. If you find you get six straight brush-offs perhaps you weren't feeling as bright as you thought. Take a break and try again tomorrow. You can do exactly the same with the small ads you see in the newspapers. Yes, some of those ads will be from other agencies, but the majority will be from private landlords. The properties are there, before your very eyes, so seize the day!

WHAT WOULD YOU THINK?

Imagine for a moment that the private landlord advertising in the paper was you. Perhaps you had been advertising the property for five or six weeks, it happens believe me, without any decent response, certainly not from suitably qualified tenants. The property is now starting to cost you money, as it will do if it's standing unoccupied. Then a cheerful person calls you up, optimistically suggesting they could perhaps let your property, and wait for it, may be even at a slightly INCREASED rental figure.

What are you going to do? Tell them to take a bunk? I wouldn't, would you? I'd want to meet them and talk to them about it some more. If you detect even the slightest chink of interest, try to fix an appointment to meet that person at their property. Don't fix the appointment for next Saturday, or some time next week; fix it for as soon as possible. What about tomorrow? What about today? What about in twenty minutes? Enthusiasm is everything.

If it means jumping in the car and going out in the rain to be there in half an hour's time, DO IT! Remember these are your first instructions and you will DO ANYTHING, within reason, to sign them up. Faint heart never won a fair landlord, or words to that effect. (Whether it's your first instruction or your fiftieth, you should be equally enthusiastic, because if you aren't, HUGE & IMPRESSIVE will be! You can be certain of that).

After all your hard work, wooing hard-hearted landlords, let's imagine you now have three or four properties on your books, including your own. You might have more, you might have less, but whatever it is, don't worry about it. You haven't even started yet.

The next task is to design some neat card ads and get them into the shop windows. You can play about with the wording to suit yourself but I suggest something along these lines.

| | | | | | | | | | | | | | | | | | | | | | | | | | | | | | | | | | | | | | | | | | | | | | | | | | | | | | | |

NEWLY ESTABLISHED PROPERTY AGENTS

Seek additional properties for rental in all areas
Good Tenants Waiting. Low Fees & No Vat
No Let – No Fee. Prompt Payment
Enquire about our Special Incentives
Ring anytime for our FREE Fact Pack and FREE rental appraisal without obligation

SOAMES HOMES
Tel: 07000 00000 (24 Hours)
| | | | | | | | | | | | | | | | | | | | | | | | | | | | | | | | | | | | | | | | | | | | | | | | | | | | | | | |

Experiment with your own cards, try two or three different designs and monitor the response from each. Concentrate in promoting headlining features such as: 'No let No fee, prompt payment, No vat, and special incentives'. These are eye catching and hopefully landlord catching too.

CAN YOU BACK UP THE CLAIMS?

Let's quickly run through the card and see. Good tenants waiting? Where are they? As soon as you place your newspaper ads you will have good tenants on your books, trust me on that. They are waiting for you out there.

Low Fees? Your fees are low, For a start there's no vat, and if you have to cut your fees by a percentage point or two, to be keener than your competitors on these initial cards then so be it. Remember, you want the instructions, and you will do anything legal and honest to get them!

No let No fee. That one's self-explanatory but it's worth emphasising again and again with new landlords. You can constantly reassure them that if you fail to let their property you will never charge them a penny. It's as simple as that. All the advertising and promotional costs will be borne by you, so the landlord has nothing to lose by instructing you. So why wouldn't they do so? There is NO reason.

Prompt payment. I'll deal with payments in more detail in the chapter covering accounting and handling cash, but this is another very important weapon in your armoury. I'll explain: It never ceases to amaze me how long some agencies hold on to the landlord's money. Why do they do that? It's not theirs. I wouldn't stand for it if I were the landlord.

One agency in my area actually paid its landlords at the end of the month following the month when the rental was collected. In other words if the rent were collected on the 2nd May that agency would pay their landlord on the 30th of June. That's an absurdity! That's eight and a half weeks! Ludicrous!

It's obvious why they do it. They are sitting on huge amounts of cash conveniently placed in a deposit account where the landlord has no entitlement to any interest. Thus the agency picks up a more than useful interest dividend at the end of every quarter.

But hanging on to the cash for so long creates a great deal of ill will towards the agency. Any agent adopting such a policy couldn't be surprised if their landlords left in droves. So pay the landlords quickly. Within 14 days at the most, 10 or even 7 days if you can manage it. Imagine for a moment if you were a landlord being paid in eight and half weeks and you heard of a new agent in the town who was paying over the rental in 7 days! Imagine that! Would you be tempted to move your business? Like hell you would! It's a great selling point; tell your potential landlords again and again. They will get: PROMPT PAYMENT!

The Free Fact Pack mentioned is the details you have already prepared and the FREE rental appraisal is exactly that. You will visit the landlord at the house and after inspecting the property you will give the landlord a free and fair appraisal of what rental you believe you can achieve, a free valuation if you prefer.

Special Incentives available. That can be anything you feel comfortable with. Perhaps a £25 or £50 off coupon that you could design on your own PC. Remember it's only for the initial landlords, as soon as you have properties on the book you can drop the promotion straight away if you want to. One new agent I knew gave the first two months management free of charge, and another start up agent gave away what he described as a free crate of wine, red or white.

The crate of wine turned out to be a box of 12 bottles he bought in the local cash and carry for £40. It was a popular promotion; he pushed it along the lines of FREE CRATE OF WINE IF YOU INSTRUCT US BEFORE THE 1st JULY. Use your imagination to come up with something the landlords won't be able to resist. Landlords are human beings. They like something FREE. Don't we all?

Lastly on the card, list your telephone number and the wonderful words, '24 Hours'. Don't worry unduly about fielding calls late into the night, you would be very unlucky to receive calls way out of office hours, and you can always leave the answering machine to field the call if you prefer. But you may well receive a call or two at 7pm or 8pm, or perhaps 8am and there's nothing wrong in that.

A lot of small landlords work for a living too, they often deal with their paperwork before they go to work or in the evenings. Many of them would be only too pleased to have the opportunity to speak to a friendly agent at 8pm to swop news and views on property matters. After all they haven't a cat in hells chance of speaking to a national company at that time of day, yet another feather in your cap, and weapon in your armoury. You're available, they aren't.

Place the cards in as many windows as you can manage. If you know any shopkeepers, ask them to put up a card FREE as a favour. You don't need to put them up for twenty weeks, four or five should be enough and sit back and wait for your replies.

WHAT TO EXPECT FROM YOUR ADVERTISING:

I'm going to tell you something now that may seem a little negative, but it's a fact of business life and it's as well you know it from day one. You will receive a very small response to your ads. Not just your card ads, but to ALL your advertising. You can absolutely rely on the fact that you will always receive LESS response to your advertising than you optimistically imagined.

But that's not a problem. It would be nice to receive dozens of replies to your card ads and hundreds from your newspaper ones, but it simply won't happen. The fact is you will probably receive only two or three replies over the monthly period from your card ads, but that doesn't matter either. It teaches you two very important things. First, that every potential client must be nurtured and fussed over as if they were your only client.

(Your clients are your business, other than any properties you might own). Secondly, that each client you sign up could earn you as much as a £1,000 per year, or more, so it doesn't matter if your efforts only produce two or three new faces, they will still cover your minimal outlay hundreds of times over.

When you are successful in signing up the clients, LOOK AFTER THEM. Remember, it is always far more cost effective to look after your existing landlords than it is to replace them with new ones.

Treat every enquiry with URGENCY
CHEERFULLY and EFFICIENTLY
Do that and you will
be invited to take the matter further

Chapter 7: Launching Your Business

Up till now your efforts have be geared towards preparing your business, but now you are ready to launch forth on the unsuspecting world with your first newspaper adverts. You only get one chance to launch your business, so do it properly, and do it well.

You will already have the newspaper publishers media packs in your possession and you will have an idea of the rates they are going to charge. All newspaper publishers calculate their small display ads on the basis of SCC. That is Single Column Centimetres. Imagine a single newspaper column, they may vary from paper to paper, but a typical one is 3 centimetres wide. A tiny box one centimetre deep down one column would equate to the quoted rate, for arguments sake £6.

If you decided your initial ads would be 3 columns wide by 5 centimetres deep you are looking at 15 centimetres, times the rate of £6. Therefore that ad would cost you £90. That's probably plus VAT too so at current rates that ad is going to cost you £105.75.

NEWSPAPER ADVERTISING IS EXPENSIVE:

You don't need to be a genius to see that newspaper advertising is not cheap, especially if it doesn't produce the necessary response, so it's imperative that you get the very best from your advertising campaign. You can do this by:

1. Heavy haggling on the rate

2. Intense concentration in dealing carefully with every call
3. Monitoring rigorously the response
4. Picking up special offers

We have already mentioned in a previous chapter about haggling with publishers. Be sure you do. Investigate the possibility of a series discounts. Many publishers offer 4 insertions for the costs of 3, or 5 for the cost of 6. Just be careful you don't book too big an ad for too long a series in a duff paper that doesn't produce the desired results.

Don't forget to mention too that you are launching a new business, demand a discount, and if you don't get one consider going somewhere else. I would NEVER book an ad in any paper, series or otherwise unless I obtained a discount or incentive of some kind. Be tough; remember at the end of the day the publisher does want your business. They hate it if you go somewhere else.

You'll find a huge discrepancy in the SCC rate between different papers. In my area one paper charges £3 per SCC, another £15, so why the huge difference? In other words a display ad in one costs five times the same size ad in another.

Of course it is all about print run, circulation. One of those papers has a circulation of 22,000, the other 140,000, so although one paper charges five times as much, it is in fact a reasonable deal as they carry 6.36 times more readers. You will clearly receive a greater response from the larger circulation paper. The question is, will you receive five or six times as much, or more?

Take a good look too at which papers are carrying the bulk of the property advertising. This is no coincidence. The chances are they have been carrying the most property advertising for many years, and the local population knows that, and always reaches for the tried and trusted Local Post when they are thinking about property and not the Local Mail. If that were the case I'd go with the established property paper every time.

Yes, there might be an argument that it may be better to be the only letting agent advertising on the Mail, but I'd rather be among the other ten agents in the Post, because that's where most potential tenants will look.

MONITOR THE RESPONSE:

Monitoring the response is most important, especially if you choose to advertise in more than one paper. If you do that, accurate monitoring will give you important clues as to where to concentrate your future firepower. It will also provide you with a statistic on exactly how much each individual response has cost.

For example if you spent £100 on an ad and you received 20 replies it's obvious that each reply has cost you £5. If you missed dealing with some of those replies because you were out or too busy, say 8 of them, that would mean the cost of the replies you picked up would have risen sharply to £8.33 each, a huge difference and another reminder of how important it is to take and nurture EVERY SINGLE REPLY. If you decide to advertise in more than one paper, don't forget to ask the callers where they saw your ad, so you can pinpoint which paper is producing the business. By doing that you can direct the bulk of your advertising spend in that direction in future.

So imagine you have researched the advertising market and have decided to place an ad in the Local Post measuring 3 columns by 7 centimetres. 21 centimetres in all but you have haggled the rate down to £5.50 so the total cost comes to £135.71 after vat has been added, but you've also managed to obtain a fifth ad free of charge after the first four have been paid for. That additional incentive has brought the cost down to £108.59 per ad.

CHOOSE YOUR WORDING CAREFULLY:

All that remains is to finalise the wording and fax it off to the newspaper. I suggest you experiment with the layout and design three or four different ads before you settle on the final choice(s).

You must remember to include all your strong points, the points that put you ahead and above the majority of your competitors. They are No Vat, No Sale No Fee, Prompt Payment, Free Fact pack, Free Appraisal, Competitive Fees, and if you are continuing with it, your SPECIAL INTRODUCTORY OFFER. Never use the word "cheap" when it comes to fees. You are certainly not cheap, competitive you may be, but never cheap! Your ad may look something like this:

||||||||||||||||||||||||||||||||||||||||||||||||||||

PROPERTY TO LET

HALTON 2 bed unf first floor flat   £495 pcm
ASHBY 3 bed unf semi det house   £595 pcm
HAMLEY 4 bed unfurn det house   £895 pcm

LANDLORDS: We have good tenants waiting for property in all areas.
No let, No fee. No vat. Prompt rental payment. Free rental appraisal
Free Fact Pack available. Ask about our special introductory offer
Please ring for more information.

TENANTS: Seeking a property in this area?
Register your requirements with us today.
No fee payable until you apply for a home.
Call us now 24 hours

BRENTS RENTS   Tel: 07000 00000
||||||||||||||||||||||||||||||||||||||||||||||||||||

ALWAYS LEAD WITH PROPERTIES:

As you can see we've led with the properties we have to let. One of these we may have picked up through a friend, one from our telephone calls to the card ads, and the third might be our own, (albeit at a huge price!) We've led on properties that we have to let because that is the main reason most people will read this page. It would be a mistake to run an ad containing no property at all. No matter what the wording was it would still look like "we're new, we haven't anything to let yet, please give us something. Please!" Be creative. Produce property to let.

When you've faxed your rough copy to the publisher they will typeset it for you at no additional expense and if you've requested it they will fax you back a proof copy of your actual ad. You can quickly check it and ring the publisher and advise them of any errors or changes that are necessary. I'd always demand a pre publication checking copy. Newspapers do make mistakes, and more often than you might think, and sometimes they are not too bothered about compensating you for them afterwards. If they printed an incorrect telephone number imagine how irritated you'd feel about that, especially on your launch week.

Once you begin to run your own ads similar to the one above you will start to pick up new properties. This is an absolute fact. Why? Because:

1. You are not charging vat
2. Your rental prices are good, especially the last one!
3. There are some desperate landlords out there, with empty property
4. Some people will always try a new face
5. Some landlords want to use every agent

WHY LANDLORDS WILL INSTRUCT YOU:

Fortunately, from the agent's point of view there are some landlords out there who are living on a knife-edge. They have perhaps extended themselves a little more than they should have. As interest rates rise you can expect to come across an ever-increasing number of stressed landlords. It's bad for them, but it's great for you. Suddenly they may have two or three properties that have become empty at the same time.

Perhaps they can't afford to meet the mortgage payments. Thus they will try each and EVERY agent in a desperate effort to let their empty houses, which is where you come in. Snap them up. They might also be attracted to your high rental quotes. Those same desperate landlords have probably already placed their houses with every agent in the district, but that doesn't matter. All that matters is that YOU now have them too.

Bear in mind that your early objective is to let the few properties you already have, but secondly and more importantly to add perhaps twice as many properties to your next advertisement.

Even if you were lucky enough to let the three properties you quoted here, and picked up three new ones, I would recommend advertising all six the following week. It will demonstrate to keen eyed landlords that you are quickly gaining instructions and becoming established. You might consider putting a NOW LET slash notice against one or two. That creates a very positive image. New properties and successful lets, and that is a recipe for success.

When landlords call, you know how you to react
Quickly, cheerfully and efficiently

Speak with a smile on your face
Make an early appointment to meet them
Be complimentary

WIDEN YOUR LAUNCH:

Beef up your business launch by designing and distributing your own colour A4 posters. A good inkjet printer will produce reasonable quality posters for very little cost.

Call in a few favours from the traders you use and ask them to put one of your posters in their windows for FREE. The newsagent where you buy your daily paper, the barbers where you have your hair cut, the pet shop where you buy your birdseed, all these kind of traders want to keep your business and will surely put up one of your posters for five or six weeks to do so. Use your imagination, keep a few posters in the car as you never know when and where you might stumble across an opportunity to display your services, but don't illegally bill post. That will only cause you grief. Ask your partner to do the same, and any other friends or relatives who own shops too.

This type of additional publicity will cost you next to nothing and it will gradually make you and your activities better known throughout the town. If you put up ten posters and picked up two new clients it would pay for your time one hundred times over.

PREPARE A PRESS RELEASE:

Speak to your local newspapers too especially the ones where you have placed the bulk of your advertising and try and wangle some editorial from them. Local papers are often stuck for news to fill out their columns and editorial is better coverage than paid for advertising because that is often shoved away on the advertising only pages. It's free!

Prepare a "Press Release" to give your launch more credibility and post a copy to all your local newspapers and radio stations. It could be along the these lines:

"Former policeman/teacher etc etc launches new local property company", or
"Local man hopes to offer employment via his new property business," or
"Local woman returns to the town and sets up new property company," or
"New Property Company opens in the city/town."

Play about with it, and you will come up with something eye-catching and memorable. Read it to your spouse, read it to your kids. They'll soon tell you if it's too cheesy.

Include your telephone number and email address in all announcements so that readers can contact you. Put a photograph in too, perhaps in front of a property, that would be a real coup.

Tell people all about it. Spread the word. Local newspapers are usually only too pleased to run a little editorial about local people setting up new enterprises, especially if it will ultimately lead to local jobs. Quite often they are desperate for snippets of news to fill their columns. Be imaginative. Be creative. You will only launch your business once and you won't have the opportunity to distribute this particular press release ever again.

DEALING WITH TENANTS FOR THE FIRST TIME:

Prepare yourself properly to deal with prospective tenants for the first time. If you are not used to dealing with clients on the telephone it might be an idea to type and print out some general notes to help you when they ring. Anyone can forget their lines when talking about a new business, especially in the early days and you will find it very helpful if you have some general notes handy to refer to when tenants call.

Tenants will ring you for one of three reasons:

- ♦ To enquire about a specific property listed
- ♦ To enquire after other properties you may have
- ♦ To register their requirements

These are the questions you would like them to answer.

- Their name and is the property for a family, a couple, or single person.
- Their address: This is most important if you want to post them details at a later date.
- Phone Number: Try and get day, evening, and mobile.
- Employed: You will need to know if they are working and what they do.
- Property Type Required: flat/ terrace /semi/ det/bung/other.
- Furnished or unfurnished: very important to save wasting time.
- When do they wish to move in?
- Pets: Most important, as some landlords will not tolerate cats and dogs.
- Length of Tenancy required: they may want 2 years or 2 months, or even 2 weeks, and you need to know which.
- Rental Figure: what range do they want pay?
- Smokers: More and more landlords require non-smoking tenants.

Some tenants are only too happy to chat and will tell you anything you want to know. Others will be reluctant to give you anything more than a name and number. At this stage, respect their views, there is little to be gained by forcing the issue. They will have to provide you with full and comprehensive details before they get anywhere near renting a property.

Never issue the full address of any property to anyone over the telephone without taking their full details and telephone numbers. We had a young man who would ring almost every Thursday from a public call box. We grew to know him quite well and he turned out to be a well-known local burglar. He was particularly interested in empty properties. Once he had the address he would call round, break into the property and steal the central heating boiler or anything else that could be detached from the building. He didn't get any addresses from us.

If someone wants an address to view a particular neighbourhood you can always give out a street name, but not the individual number. We never issued house numbers until we were confident it was a bona fide enquiry and the prospective tenant wished to book an accompanied viewing of the house.

Far and away the best policy to adopt when dealing with potential tenants is to talk to them as if they are long lost friends, courteous and helpful. Try and put across that you are working for their benefit in an effort to get them fixed up. You will make a great deal more headway by adopting these friendly tactics rather than an inquisitorial attitude by bellowing one question after another in monotone, what I call the name, rank, number, syndrome.

Of course you are NOT working for the benefit of the tenant, you are working on behalf of the landlord, representing their interests, trying to find the best tenant for them at the best rental figure. By doing that successfully you will achieve results for the most important person involved in this whole enterprise, YOU! It's worth reminding yourself of that now and again.

From that first advertisement typically you could receive twenty replies from prospective tenants, half of which may well be suitable for a property somewhere. You could also typically expect to receive calls from around four or five landlords in the week that passes before your next advertisement appears. Don't forget to fuss over every single reply, especially the landlord enquiries, because they are the source of the majority of your future business.

Which brings us neatly to the next chapter, how to best woo and convert landlords to deal with you. It's an interesting and challenging task, but armed with my expertise of visiting hundreds and hundreds of landlords, you will be well equipped to win the day.

Prepare yourself to speak to tenants
Design your own form incorporating your questions
Talk to them as if they were a friend

Chapter 8: Wooing the Landlord Animal

Landlords can be likened to the animals of the African plain; they come in all shapes, sizes, colours, ages, and temperament.

In the old days landlords were pigeonholed into a stereotype of a late middle-aged man, probably with a beard and grasping hands. I suspect that was never the case, and it certainly isn't today. Your landlord is more likely to be an attractive professional woman in her twenties, or a whiz kid businessman in his thirties.

Recently I experienced a huge increase in Chinese landlords and very good they are too. I have always found them excellent to do business with, honest and straight, polite and loyal. If you give them a good deal and great service, they will undoubtedly recommend you to their aunts and uncles, and before you know it you will be representing Mr and Mrs Wang, Chang, Wu, Chu, Soo, and Lu too.

I did, and they were among the best landlords I ever dealt with. Some of them couldn't even speak English but once I'd built a successful relationship with them, they never went anywhere else. The great thing about them was they kept acquiring more and more property and would ring me up and triumphantly announce: "we have another one, you wannit?" I wannit!

One of the reasons behind their spending sprees was a huge influx of capital from Hong Kong where property prices are much higher than here. The Chinese, as everyone knows have always made excellent business people and they all seemed intent on building up property portfolios at a record rate. Long may it continue!

MEETING LANDLORDS:

So the point I am trying to make is, there is no such thing as a typical landlord. When you are fortunate enough to be invited to visit a landlord make an appointment as early as you can and try and ascertain whether the property you are meeting him or her at, is the property they are considering letting, or their own home. That's most important and I'll tell you why in a minute.

Most landlords will meet you at the property that is to be let; but many will invite you into their own homes. Imagine you have an appointment to visit a landlord at his home at 2pm the following day. The first point to remember is to BE EARLY! I don't mean knock on the door early, just get into the area promptly, just in case the traffic is bad. Think about it this way, the landlord may well have invited three different agents to visit him at hourly intervals. Imagine two are late and one is on the nail, who do you think will get the instruction? Precisely!

I liked to knock on the door at exactly the time the appointment was made. There is nothing more satisfying than being invited into the hall as the clock is loudly chiming the time. The landlord will notice your punctuality, you can be sure of that.

Offer your hand, if they wish to shake it, they will. Incidentally my Chinese friends were never keen to shake hands and after a while I gave up proffering mine. If the landlord does offer his hand, shake it firmly and briefly. Never offer a wet fish of a handshake, it's a real turn off, and never bone-crush his hand as a statement of how strong and tough you are. As in many things the happy medium is the preferred route.

Don't sit down until you are invited to do so. A small point perhaps, but some people notice manners more than most. Always wipe your feet, especially if it is wet and muddy. You may have sent your fact pack ahead in the post, but always bring another one just in case the landlord wishes to go over a few points or has lost his copy. Try and relax, try and smile, be friendly, and treat this person as you would a wealthy relative. Answer any questions carefully and confidently and don't forget to emphasis your USP's.

EMPHASISE YOUR USP'S:

What are USP's? Unique Selling Points. You know what your USP's are. No vat, No let - No fee, No advertising costs, free rental appraisal, competitive fees, and perhaps most importantly of all you can state categorically that you will turn over the rental payment within 10 days (or whatever time you have set). Just make sure you adhere to that. There's nothing worse than an agent promising to pay rental within 10 days, only for the landlord to be still waiting 30 days later.

By the way just make sure you word that correctly. You are not promising to turn over the rental in 10 days from the date it is due, say the first of the month, you are promising to turn it over within 10 days of IT BEING COLLECTED. That's an important difference, because the tenant may sometimes pay a little late. Your USP's may not be unique individually but put together the package you are offering will be.

If you are competing against big national agents, you can do so with confidence. They will never be able to compete with you on flexibility of terms. You can change your prices, or anything else, at the drop of a hat. They could need seven committee meetings and refer to Head Office before they could change theirs.

I mentioned before about trying to ascertain whether the property you were meeting at was the property to be let or not. The reason for that is simple. If it were the property to be let, you have an easy and early opportunity to value the rental figure. Firstly you could drive past and check out the neighbourhood and the exterior condition of the property. Secondly you may notice two or three similar properties in the neighbourhood to let. You could hurry back to the office and check out the rental figures. It's obviously much easier to reach an accurate rental figure if you already know what three other similar properties in the same road are on the market for.

DISCLOSING YOUR VALUATION:

When a landlord asks for your valuation give it to them straight. Don't prevaricate. You can perhaps justify your figure by adding "number 19 is on the market for £550 but that one is not centrally heated, yours is a slightly better property hence the figure of £595". What you are really telling them is that you have done your research, you have your finger on the pulse, and you know what is going on. You haven't simply plucked a figure out of thin air and hoped for the best.

The landlord should be impressed. Hopefully he or she has liked your demeanour, your valuation was spot on, and they were particularly pleased with your trump cards of no vat and early payment. They were so pleased they might even instruct you there and then to get on with it. That is not unusual. I have been instructed hundreds of times on site within ten minutes of meeting a complete stranger.

I have been issued with keys on numerous occasions to properties worth over half a million pounds within ten minutes of meeting a complete stranger for the first time. It's a nice feeling to realise they had enough confidence in you for them to do that, and you will too. The more often you are instructed, the more confident you will become in the future.

If they are instructing you to let their property it is important to agree the viewing arrangements. They will be one of these:

1. The landlord will give you a key, be sure to check if there is an alarm system, if there is, make sure you obtain the code.

2. The landlord will meet any potential viewers on site. In that case make sure you attend too. If you don't, the landlord might strike a private deal behind your back with the tenant. (They wouldn't do that would they? They might if you gave them the chance!)

3. The landlord will arrange for someone else to open up. Again, you should attend. Why? Because you can hand the potential tenant an application form. You might even be able to collect the application fee there and then. If you do, it will be the first fee you ever collect. Money is the incentive. Go to all viewings.

NOTES ON BURGLAR ALARMS:

Burglar alarms are very commonplace and increase the security of any property, but they can be a nuisance for agents, especially if you forget about the alarm. There is nothing worse than opening a property with a keen viewer on your shoulder, only to hear that beep-beep-beep as you realise that you have forgotten about the alarm or worse, that the landlord had not bothered to tell you about it. In some areas perhaps half of all houses have alarms, so always go prepared.

Most alarms are one of two types, either code, usually four digits, or key, where you simply insert the key in the alarm and turn it off. Here's a tip if you unexpectedly hear the dreaded beeps and have no code:

Most codes are either a famous date, the landlord's birthday for example, which you are unlikely to know, or the one date that everyone knows, 1066. You will be surprised at how often that is the code. It's worth a try. But there is another code that comes up time and time again. That is 0123. Why? Because that is the default code that the system is supplied with and many owners never reset it. So try 0123 and you might be lucky. If it's a key type, many cheaper systems use a small key like a filing cabinet key. In fact they are so alike that they will often do the job for you. That might be worth a try too, so if you have a similar key on your ring, try it

If that fails you should be able to sort the problem via your mobile phone and hopefully before the police arrive!

CONFIRMING INSTRUCTIONS:

Once instructed, return to your office and write a letter to the landlord, in duplicate, confirming their instruction to you to let the property. Confirm the ASKING rental, and remind the landlord that a Gas Safety Certificate will be necessary, (lots more on that topic later). Start an individual file for the property, those large multi coloured cardboard document wallets are excellent for the purpose. You can place copies of all correspondence in the file as you proceed, you can note any telephone calls you make on there relating to the property and you can keep all relevant paperwork together in one place.

Make sure before you take the matter any further you have the landlord sign the second copy of your letter and return it to you as an acknowledgement. This is most important, without it you have nothing in writing that instructs you to proceed. If you sign up for one of the software packages, these letters are all automatically generated.

You may be instructed there and then, but the chances are you won't be. Return to the office and hope the phone rings over the next day or three. Even after that you don't need to write the property off. I have been instructed up to nine months after visiting a landlord. He explained he'd been decorating the house and he liked to do it at his own speed. But if you don't hear anything further, or are confident you failed to win his or her trust, try and analyse why you didn't get the instruction, especially if the very next week you notice the property appearing in your rival's advertisement.

REASONS FOR FAILURE:

Why did you fail to land the instruction? Could it be one of these?

1. Your rivals valued it higher (even if it was unrealistic). There's nothing you could have done about that. If it's overvalued you can be sure it will be tricky to let. If they struggle to let it, which they will, it may well come back to you.
2. The landlord didn't like you. (Hey it happens, none of us likes everyone, that's human nature). Forget about it. There are more fish in the sea.
3. You stumbled over answering questions. (Well you won't do that again will you?)
4. The landlord got cold feet about letting at all. (Yep, that happens too, there's nothing you can do about that either).

71

5. You were late, (that is unforgivable!)
6. The landlord was a timewaster and really only wanted to pick your brains before trying to let it himself. (Yes, that happens too sometimes, and you will probably recognise it when it does. All you can do is be helpful and polite and leave as quickly as you can to pursue other business).

If you can successfully analyse why you didn't get the instruction, you will improve your chances of being successful next time.

HOW TO IMPRESS YOUR LANDLORDS:

You can impress your landlords by being:

1. On time
2. Cheerful and optimistic, smile
3. Never proffer a limp handshake, nor a bone-cruncher
4. Shine your shoes, and look smart
5. Avoid garlic breath – and alcoholic fumes too
6. Give him or her your undivided attention; turn off your mobile phone
7. Be complimentary, but not fawning, about their house, their children and pets
8. Emphasise your USP's, be enthusiastic
9. Do your homework

In the next section we'll look in more detail at valuing properties and preparing property information sheets. It's an important task, and it needs to be carried out accurately.

Chapter 9: Rental Valuations & Property Spec Sheets

There is a lot of bumph written about valuing property for rental purposes as if there were some accurate equation based on the square footage times the length of the tenancy, or some such crazy mathematical formula.

That may be the case in valuing properties for sale in Knightsbridge, but for rentals, in my opinion, no such formula exists. The value of a property for rental purposes is precisely the same as for anything else. It is worth what you can persuade someone to pay for it. And I don't mean to sign a contract at a certain figure, I mean to actually PAY THE CASH!

ESTABLISHING THE ASKING RENTAL FIGURE:

Setting the property rental value with confidence comes with experience. The more you do it, the easier it becomes. And don't forget this applies just as much to valuing your own property as it does for others. If you are unsure about a valuation, you can always say to the landlord: "did you have a figure in mind?" I personally don't care for that tack as it smacks of a lack of confidence, but occasionally it might be the right path if you are especially unsure.

Most landlords will have a figure they want, and many will tell you, but there are always those that say, "You're the expert, you tell me". That's fair enough. They are right. The fact is, if you've done your homework, as you should have done, you will KNOW an accurate figure BEFORE you visit the house. You can always adjust it up or downward once you have inspected the inside of the property.

At least you won't have the problem a friend of mine had; he's an Estate Agent in Canford Cliffs in the leafy suburbs of Bournemouth. He was invited to value a modern home on the trendy Sandbanks peninsula. Fortunately the vendor was a friend of his and when he was asked for his valuation my friend said: "it's a difficult one I could be way out here".

Before he could say any more his friend started laughing and told him they'd already had three agents around the property. One had valued the house at £1.35 million, the second at £1.6 million and the third at £1.95 million! A difference of £600,000 between the top and bottom valuations! Imagine that? Being an estate agent and being £600,000 out! It doesn't bear thinking about. At least on rentals, even if you are out, you won't be that much out!!

You can also adjust your suggested figure, for that is all it is, up or down depending on market conditions. For example if there's a lot of empty property on the market and it's not shifting, it would make sense to value it slightly lower. Explain to the landlord why you have done so. On the other hand if the market was strong and properties were shifting quickly, you could afford to be more bullish and value it slightly higher than you normally might. Don't forget, there are other good reasons to value it as highly as you can.

Firstly if you can obtain a higher figure you will cement your relationship with the landlord, and secondly, remember you are working for a percentage fee. 10% of £900 is clearly better than 10% of £800. It may only be £10 per month more for you, but that's £120 a year. If you did that fifty times, as you may well do, it begins to add up. Concentrate on increasing your fee income, and you don't need to increase your prices to do so. If you can do that, you will achieve your goals that much quicker.

UPDATE YOUR INTELLIGENCE:

Continue to monitor ALL properties that are for rental in your area. If you do that, you will always have your finger on the pulse when it comes to valuations. I confidently predict that within one month you will be happily and accurately valuing properties, providing you have done your homework. Believe me, anyone can do it.

MAKE NOTES & LOTS OF THEM!

When you visit properties always take your diary and make copious notes. There is nothing worse than an agent having to ring the landlord back and say: "remind me again, was it centrally heated?" It makes you look a complete Wally, and worse, incompetent. If you make accurate notes you will not need to ring back.

These points are most important to note:

- Furnished or Unfurnished? It could affect the value, and the tenant.
- Double glazed and centrally heated?
- Is there a shower, second bathroom?
- Off road parking? Garage?
- Is there a fitted kitchen?
- Number of bedrooms of course, similarly reception rooms?
- When available? Length of time available? One year? Two years?
- Alarmed? Key or Code?
- Are the gas and electricity meters quarterly or coin? That is important, as it is to ascertain who supplies the services?

- Is there a garden? Who has access, especially important on flats? Is there a gardener? Is there a garage? Is the garage empty? Most are not!

- Are there curtain rails? If not try and persuade the landlord to put some up. Not many tenants want to start messing around with curtain rails.

- What is the state of repair of the property? Don't be afraid to ask the landlord to deal with essential maintenance, especially anything to do with gas and electric. Cracked windows should be dealt with too. Have a look at the outside of the property as well. Are there any overhanging tiles that could fall on visiting tenants, or on you? If so, insist they are repaired.

- Is there a banister on the stairs? There should be.

- Is there plumbing for a washing machine and dishwasher?

- Is there a modern fitted kitchen and bathroom? If so, make an issue of it in your descriptions.

- Will the landlord accept smokers and pets? That's most important, as many people will not.

For the most part it is simple common sense. You need to find out the things that you would want to know if you were renting the house yourself. I find the best way to ensure you don't miss anything is to design your own easy to follow checklist. Include all the above features and any others you deem necessary, that way you will never miss a thing.

It is not necessary to measure the rooms. I don't know of any letting agent who does. It would add extra work for no benefit, and it could provide the nitpickers and compensation seekers an easy opening to make a complaint against you. You know the kind of thing. "You said the living room was 14'6" when it's only 14'2". We want a deduction in the rent". Who needs that kind of hassle? And believe me it does happen

WRITING A PROPERTY SPEC SHEET:

When you return to the office you can write a brief description of the property. My advice would be to keep it short and simple, to the point, and above all, accurate. Avoid flowery language, the word "gorgeous" has no place in any property description, and never say anything that is obviously untrue. Your description could read something like this.

"An unfurnished 3 bedroom semi detached house benefiting from gas central heating, part double-glazing, garage and spacious gardens. The accommodation comprises hall, lounge, sitting room, modern fitted kitchen, 3 bedrooms and modern bathroom. Outside there is a detached garage, ample off road parking and lawned enclosed gardens to the rear. The property is available now for 12 months with an extension possible thereafter. No pets or smokers please. Please ring our office for more information and to make an early appointment to view".

That's 84 words if my maths is correct. If you exceed over say 150 words, on a letting, you're probably including too much detail. That's really all you need, a basic description. If the prospective tenant requires further details on any aspect of the property, they can ask you about it. After all, you do want them to ring.

TAKE PICTURES:

Don't forget while you are at the property to take several photographs of the property with your digital camera. The main photograph should be of the front elevation. If it isn't, and you use it on your spec sheets, you must say so. Interior photographs may also be taken if required. Interior photographs can also act as an important check at a later date as to the condition and content of the inside of the house. Always ask your landlord's permission if it is in order to photograph the property. It is polite and courteous to do so.

Even if you are not initially instructed, you will have the pictures on file saved for a later date. With the advent of digital cameras you do not have to worry about expensive development costs, so you can go a little mad. In the early days you may like to take twenty or more pics, once you look at them on your computer you can always delete the dodgy ones. By taking a good number of shots you will always find some good ones amongst them. If there is a strong sun shining directly at you, you may need to call back a little later.

With a little ingenuity you will quickly be able to produce neat accurate property spec sheets in full colour using the benefit of modern inexpensive technology. Just because you are small, new and independent, does not mean you shouldn't be able to look professional and competent. Learn how to email the spec sheets too, as an attachment, together with colour photos. That will impress your landlords and tenants alike. Use modern technology to your advantage. It is a tool Use it.

GOOD SPELLING IS PROFESSIONALISM:

Make sure your spelling is up to the mark. You can always enlist the help of the spell checker, though spell checkers are not always to be trusted. My spell checker for example would not recognise the word Liverpool no matter what I did. It consistently wanted to re-write it as Liverwort! Here's a short spelling test.

Which of these property related words are spelt incorrectly?

Accomodation
Extention

Tennant
Leese
Negociated
Mezanine
Tennancy
Rentalls
Conservatary
Double-glased
Propperty
Houseing
Bennefits

Answer: They are <u>ALL</u> incorrect.
Get it right? Well, of course you did.

Why is spelling so important anyway? In a word: professionalism. If you can't be bothered to ensure you spell your blurbs correctly, what confidence can the landlord have that you will take the time to prepare your paperwork accurately? Indeed what confidence could he or she have in anything you do? Some words can have a completely different meaning when spelt slightly wrongly. That could be an important factor on a tenancy agreement. Accommodation is the word that property companies spell incorrectly time and time again. Make sure you don't. It's easy to remember. Two m's and two c's. That's it.

Make the effort to get it right, check everything and keep improving. Everyone can improve, pay attention to detail, it will eventually be that fact that marks you out from your rivals. There's nothing better than to hear a landlord say: "your paperwork is always so well done!" Excellent. That's the objective. Everything you do is, " so well done".

Incidentally I've just noticed my spell checker passed seven of those ten words as being correct! In my best Victor Meldrew voice, I do not believe it!

Chapter 10: Meeting & Interviewing Prospective Tenants

Meeting and interviewing prospective tenants for the first time can be an interesting experience. It's a fact that absolutely anyone from a member of the Royal family downward may require to rent a home at some stage in their lives. If you have a mental picture of prospective tenants as somehow being downmarket fallen on hard times layabouts, then get rid of the picture. It might have been true once, it certainly isn't now.

Robert Maxwell, when he was alive, rented his mansion from Oxford City Council. He described it as the best council house in all England. The Duke of Marlborough rents Blenheim Palace from the Crown, albeit for the hefty rental figure of £1 a year on condition they never pay late! Well they wouldn't would they? People who rent property should not be categorised as any different to people who own their homes, after all, they might be a hundred times wealthier than the people living next door.

Imagine the picture, you have advertised a property, perhaps that two-bedroom first floor flat at £495 per month. You received six calls enquiring about the flat, three of whom would like to view the property.

Try to book the viewings at the same time, by same time I don't mean at precisely the same moment, but say twenty minutes apart, that is usually enough. It doesn't take long to view an unfurnished flat. You could arrange them all at exactly the same time if you really wanted to, or were pushed for time, but I wouldn't recommend it. If you did, you couldn't give each viewer the attention they deserve.

Nor could you answer their questions if someone else was bombarding your other ear.

Imagine you booked the viewings for 2pm, 2.20pm and 2.40pm. By block booking it has saved you having to go out a second or even a third time. Arrive early and pick up newspapers and junk mail that will inevitably be littering the hallway. If it's in any way dingy put the lights on, especially in common parts. Lights are always lit in show houses, have you noticed? And for a good reason, they show off the property to the best advantage. Learn from them. Do what they do, especially if it works.

It's also a good idea to have some neat business cards printed. When the tenants arrive, hand them a card. It reassures the prospective tenant you are who you say you are. They may also hand the card to someone else later on, if they are not interested in the property themselves; it's a useful source of free advertising.

There's not a great deal to see in an empty flat and I'd recommend you invite them to wander around unaccompanied, as most people prefer to do that. If you feel uncomfortable with that, or for some reason uncomfortable with the tenant, you could always show them round but you don't need to announce: "this is the kitchen, this is the bathroom". People are not stupid.

PERSONAL SECURITY:

Here's an important word of warning. Never turn your back on the viewer. Why? Well you have absolutely no idea who they are. Invite them to go on ahead of you, where you can see them. They may have told you they were a teacher from the local junior school, but at that stage you only have their word for it. The truth is, they could be anyone, someone with mental health problems who had recently been returned to the community, or an axe murderer, unlikely I agree, but not an impossibility. Never turn your back on tenants until you learn more about them.

Remember, your security is paramount. And your staff's, when you begin recruiting. I'm sure I don't need to remind you of the dreadful Susan Lamplugh case to illustrate my point as to what could happen, no matter how long the odds may be, and this applies equally to men as well as women. Remain vigilant and alert at all times until that person is off the premises. If you can, tell someone where you are going, and what time you'll be back. Always take your mobile phone with you, and make sure it is charged. Don't take unnecessary risks, however tiny they may seem.

ALWAYS ISSUE APPLICATION FORMS:

When a tenant has finished viewing any property they'll almost certainly ask you questions. I always make a point of giving them an application form, whether they are interested in the property or not, together with a sheet of general terms and conditions including information about the fee payable by them. The point of doing this is, even if they are not interested in that particular property, they will have your letterheads, terms of business, and telephone numbers readily to hand, and they may well ring you back in a day or two, or a week or two.

They might also share an existing property with other potential tenants, they may for example be residing in a nurse's home where people are coming and going all the time, and if anyone else sees your name and number they might ring you too. It's all about FREE ADVERTISING and PROMOTING YOUR BUSINESS. Getting yourself known is not just an expensive newspaper advertising campaign. Word of mouth is, if anything more important, and far cheaper!

NO SHOWS:

Of all the appointments the public make, you can expect one in five to be a no show. Some people will ring in and cancel, and some will not. If you ring those that didn't bother to show, they will either not answer the telephone, or mumble some excuse, either way an apology is a rare thing from people like that. All you can do is bite your lip, shrug your shoulders, and think that if they couldn't be bothered to cancel the appointment, what sort of tenant would they have made, especially when it came to honouring rental payments? You are probably better off without them.

Some agents ring all viewers an hour or two prior to the viewing to check if they are going and you might like to try that. If it cuts down the number of no shows and thus reduces the amount of time wasted, it will be well worth it.

COMPLETING & COLLECTING APPLICATION FORMS:

Many potential tenants are under pressure to find new accommodation quickly. Perhaps their existing tenancy agreement is rapidly coming to an end and they have been served with a notice to vacate the property. Perhaps they are taking up a new work appointment and need to sort their accommodation prior to that. But whatever the reason, it is not unusual for keen tenants to fill out an application form there and then, at the viewing, and hand it to you before they leave.

This works well too, because not only can you help them complete the application form accurately and completely, you can also collect the application fee at the same time. Driving away with a completed application form and the accompanying fee of £100 or whatever it is, tucked into your pocket serves to inspire you onward to greater things.

Remember, this money is yours, it is not the landlords, and it is not returnable. (I'll come back to that in a minute.)

Make sure that on the application form it clearly states that any SECURITY DEPOSIT payable will be returned within 14 days of the tenant leaving the property, by CHEQUE to their new address, providing the rental account is up to date and the property is returned in good condition. This is most important and we'll discuss why it is so important later in the book.

While you are with the prospective tenant take the opportunity to quiz them about their circumstances and employment. You can often learn as much about someone in five minutes relaxed conversation, as you can from any amount of written information on application forms, or by taking up formal references. You will learn to gain a feel for people. You will often gain an inkling when they are telling fibs. Do tenants tell fibs? Yes, unfortunately some of them do! Personal intuition can be as good a referencing tool as any number of glowing written references. After ten years experience I'd back my intuition against written references every time.

While you are with them it's a good idea to picture in your own mind how the letting will pan out three or four months down the line. Imagine for instance how it would be if this tenant failed to pay the rent. How would you feel about chasing that person? If you thought you might feel in any way intimidated, or that the tenant might be in any way troublesome, perhaps a small warning red light should be going off in your mind.

TAKING UP REFERENCES:

As soon as you return to the office start the referencing procedure. Don't put it off till tomorrow, regardless of when the tenant is seeking to start the tenancy, DO IT NOW!

It doesn't matter one jot whether you are considering the tenant for one of your own properties or one of your clients, there are five references you should consider taking up. They are:

1. Employer's reference
2. Current landlord's reference
3. Previous landlord's reference, if current one less than a year
4. Banker's reference
5. Credit reference

EMPLOYER'S REFERENCE:

The employer's reference is to ascertain whether the applicant is actually employed, and if so, is employed where they say they are. Some employers will tell you a great deal of information about their employee without you ever having to ask for it. Other employers ever mindful of the data protection act will tell you almost nothing. Pay particular attention to confirming that the employment is full time. There are many people employed in December who are not in January, post office sorting workers for example, even professional Santa Clauses.

LANDLORD'S REFERENCES:

The current landlord's reference will ascertain that the applicant lives where they say they live. It may also reveal comments about the applicant's payment record. The previous landlord's reference is the same, and additionally proves the applicant's conduct over a longer period. The landlord's references also serve as a potential introduction for you to new landlords. Don't let the opportunity go to waste. Jot down the landlord's telephone number in your contact book. Don't let them pass you by without at least speaking to them once about other property matters, besides the tenant you are currently referencing. Be bold; ask them if they have anything empty. Most will tell you if they have.

BANKER'S REFERENCE:

The banker's reference is the one that most landlords ask about, and yet in my opinion is the one I put the least store by. In all the time I took up banker's references the only statement they ever made was "good for normal commitments". What the heck does that mean? One gentleman whom the bank described as "good for normal commitments" went bankrupt six weeks after I moved him into an apartment. So how good was that exactly?

I have never seen a detrimental banker's reference, ever, and I would question the whole point of carrying one out. Worse still, you have to pay for them these days, and some banks charge as much as £25 up front for typing out a brief letter on a single piece of paper. That's ridiculous! If you decide not to take up banker's references and a landlord asks you why you did not, tell them they are not worth the paper they are written on, because they aren't!

CREDIT REFERENCE:

The final reference is the credit reference and this is very relevant. You will need to sign up with one of the property credit referencing bureaux such as Homelet or Letsure. You'll find their addresses and telephone numbers in the trade directory at the end of this book.

They will of course charge you for the references, normally around £8 or £9 for a basic report, or up to £25 for a comprehensive one. These costs are borne by the agent and are paid out of the application fee. That is another very good reason why it should not be returned. Why should you stand the tenant's search fees? Of course you shouldn't. You are a professional business, not a charity. These references are usually based on a scoring principle with a pass mark around 140.

I have seen scores well over 300, and as low as 2. Anything over 140 is a pass. The references will show up county court judgments, loan defaults, and similar financial problems in the applicant's background. If a person doesn't have CCJ's (County Court Judgement's) or loan defaults, and is on the current voter's roll, they will almost certainly pass with flying colours. I always had great faith in credit references. In all my time letting property, I very rarely experienced a financial problem with anyone who had passed a credit reference. I often did, with people who failed. If I had to rely on one reference alone, it would be this one.

Once you've filled out the credit reference form I recommend you fax it, or email, to the agency immediately. Speed is of the essence. You can't rely on snail mail any more. Depending on the service you've signed up for, you can often obtain a reply within the hour and that might be important.

COMPLETE THE REFERENCING PROCEDURE QUICKLY:

Some letting agencies tell their potential tenants, especially the larger longer established ones, that it takes a week to process an application. Poppycock! Absolute balderdash! Do these people live in the modern age? The fact is that with modern technology ALL the references can be obtained on the very day the application has been received by the agent, if the agent shows the necessary urgency to obtain them.

And if not as quick as that, certainly within twenty-four hours. Remember, it is in your interest, and your landlord's interest to process and pass or fail the application as quickly as possible. Why? Because all the while the proposed deal is up in the air, the tenant has the option of walking away saying "I've found something better and cheaper". Just because the potential tenant has applied to you, it doesn't necessarily mean they have stopped looking elsewhere too.

You need to know as soon as possible whether the tenant has failed, because if they have, you should be concentrating your efforts on finding someone else. As a final check you can do my 'Me-Me-Me' test. What's the Me-Me-Me test? It's simple. Say to yourself in all honesty, would you be happy to put this person in YOUR house? If the answer is "yes", well fine, crack on with it, but if the answer is "no", how could you possibly justify putting this person in someone else's house? There's something wrong there somewhere. There could be trouble ahead.

Once you receive an acceptable landlord's reference, credit reference, and employer's reference, faxed copies will do, you can then speak to the landlord and tell him or her that you have successfully located a fully referenced tenant and check with them if it is in order to proceed. At that stage they may well ask you a few questions about the tenant, such as "do they have any pets", "or are they smokers?"

This may be a way they have of quickly checking whether you have indeed done your homework properly. If you don't know, don't guess. Tell them you will double check and find out. Most landlords want to let their property as soon as possible, the last thing they need is for a house or flat to stand empty, so once you tell them the tenant has passed the referencing procedure, nine times out of ten the landlord will say, "well done, get 'em in!"

Another reason to double check with the landlord before you proceed is because they might have instructed another agents to let the same house. I'm sorry to say it often happens that a property that may have been sticking for a week or two suddenly becomes let by two or even three different agencies at the same time, sometimes even to the same bunch of tenants! Clearly if that's the situation you need to know about it immediately. It's sods law, there's nothing you can do about it, but put it to the back of your mind and concentrate on the next deal.

TENANTS WHO FAIL REFERENCING:

What do you do if a tenant fails a reference? All is not lost. You need to examine why they have failed any particular reference. The first thing you must do is not to ignore a failure. You have a duty of care towards the landlord. If you steam ahead and put a tenant into a property knowing full well they have failed their checks, you would be taking a huge risk, and would be storing up big trouble for yourself.

Yes you may be blinded by the nice fee that you are so close to pocketing, especially if you have experienced a quiet month, but:

NEVER PLACE A TENANT INTO A PROPERTY WHO HAS FAILED THEIR REFERENCES

Remember, the landlord might ask to see the references at any time, as they are entitled to do. What are you going to say? "Oh sorry I didn't notice it was a failure!" It won't wash, and you could find yourself on the end of a very expensive legal claim, not to mention losing a very good client.

So what can you do in the event of failure? If the tenant has failed the credit check because of one CCJ, perhaps for non-payment of the council tax from some year's ago. You need to ring the tenant and ask them the full circumstances of the default. If they can't or won't discuss the matter, I would reject them there and then. If any tenant says they didn't know they had a CCJ, you can be fairly sure they are telling fibs. But it isn't difficult to end up with a CCJ; you might be surprised at how many people are wandering around out there with them. Anyone can forget about a certain bill and end up with a stain on their record. A whole string of them mind, is a completely different matter.

GUARANTORS:

The usual way of proceeding further would be to ask the prospective tenant to provide a GUARANTOR. A guarantor is someone who will sign the tenancy agreement AS WELL as the tenant and who will be responsible for each and every term on that agreement INCLUDING a responsibility to pay the rental, should the tenant not do so. The guarantor would also be equally responsible for the property to be returned in good condition when the tenancy ends.

It is a big responsibility being a guarantor, and many people will not take it on, unless they have the utmost confidence in the tenant. A guarantor should ideally be employed, and a homeowner. In that case you know if the tenant defaults they would have the wherewithal to honour their obligations. If a guarantor treats the matter as a complete joke by saying something like: "I'll sign anything you want, you won't get a thing from me", and yes, that does happen, reject them immediately.

Reference the guarantor including, a credit check, just as you would a tenant. If the guarantor fails the credit check as well, bright red lights should be going off in your mind. Guarantors are usually parents, close relatives, or spouses and ex spouses. I would be very suspicious of anyone else standing as a guarantor without good reason. You have to ask yourself, why are they standing as a guarantor? Would you stand as a guarantor for someone you weren't related to? Unlikely I suspect. It could hit you hard in the pocket. Why would you take the risk?

A young lady recently applied for a tenancy on a flat of mine, she failed her credit check by a big margin. She'd viewed the property with her father. I rang him up and asked him if he would stand as a guarantor. He laughed and replied "no thanks". What does that say? If her own father wouldn't stand as a guarantor, what kind of tenant was she going to make? Needless to say I passed on that one, and I hope you would have done too.

No matter how keen you, or your landlord is, to fill a property, there is always another potential tenant around the corner. If you are struggling to get pass references on a particular tenant, don't be shy to reject them. Even if it's your brother, as once happened to an agent I know! If you fill your properties with slightly border line tenants, or worse, you will not only gain a reputation for supplying dodgy tenants, but you will also be storing up untold problems for yourself in the future.

BAD TENANTS WASTE TIME:

Believe me, one bad tenant can take up more of your time than fifty good ones, and they also serve towards taking your eye off the ball, which should be firmly fixed upon obtaining and filling more property, not chasing around the wastrels of this world. The place for wastrels is in the competition's property, not yours.

There is one thing you can certainly rely on, every agency sooner or later will accommodate a bad tenant, it happens to everyone. Perhaps you saw a recent Tenants from Hell programme on the TV where an up market ARLA letting agent put a tenant into a house, and the tenant paid one month's rental and then nothing else, ever again.

The tenant, who it turned out was an experienced defaulter, used every excuse and trick in the book, including issuing a string of rubber cheques, to remain in the property and it was over a year before the agent and the owner finally gained possession of the house. The landlord, a lady who only owned the one property, was forced into selling the house to cover her debts.

So every agent, no matter how professional, no matter how careful, no matter how diligent, can and will have the odd bad tenant. There are ways and means of dealing with that situation, and I will be covering that later in the book.

So the lesson is, if the references aren't good enough, get a reputable guarantor. If they can't come up with a good guarantor, reject them, simple as that. The only landlords who may accept tenants with bad records are landlords with poor quality run down property.

I have known landlords who really didn't care who was in their property providing they were filled. This is all very well providing you make it clear to those landlords that the tenant had failed their referencing right from the outset. Put it in writing to the landlord, with a little warning, so they can't come back to you at a later date and pretend they didn't know, because they might, if they have the chance.

HOUSING BAD TENANTS IS A TIME BOMB YOU CAN DO WITHOUT:

But if that is the case be warned, you may still be storing up great trouble for yourself in the future, because the landlord will still expect you to chase up overdue payments if the tenant defaults, and this is very time consuming.

If a potential tenant is at any time hostile, difficult, intimidating or disrespectful, in any way towards you, the property, or the landlord, before the let is agreed and before they are issued with the keys, imagine what they could be like after they have moved in. If a tenant is difficult and disrespectful before they move in, at a time when they are supposedly on their best behaviour, a very large warning flashing light should go off in your mind. If a potential tenant were disrespectful to any party prior to completing, I would bin them immediately. Find someone else. And remember, you can ditch a tenant at any point right up until the tenancy is signed and the initial cash paid. After that point, it is an entirely different ball game.

I once had a tenant who passed all his referencing but upon a second final inspection of the property just prior to signing and paying he began to become noticeably rude and aggressive. He started to damage the fitted kitchen before my very eyes. He pulled the doors off the hinges, ostensibly to show me how poor condition it was in, he removed the beading, admittedly slightly loose, from around the worktops. I saw him in a wholly different light, and I did not like what I saw.

I don't know who was the more surprised, the tenant or the landlord, when I cancelled the letting on the spot. I refused to take any money from him and ushered him from the house. He flushed red and bristled like an angry dog. He threatened to sue me for breach of contract, but as I pointed out to him, he didn't have a contract, they were still, thankfully, nestling unsigned in my briefcase.

He flew away from the house, bleating that I hadn't heard the last of it. But I had. I never heard a thing from him ever again, and successfully let the property to a lovely music teacher the very next day. A solicitor friend of mine later mentioned that after all that he might have had a case, but I doubt it.

TELL TENANTS RESULTS QUICKLY:

If a potential tenant fails the referencing procedure, you must ring them as soon as you can and tell them that is the case, and that you cannot proceed further. They will probably feign surprise that they had a CCJ, but the fact is that people who have CCJ's almost certainly know full well they have, and just hope that you won't do your job properly and discover them.

Some tenants will shout at you and demand their fee back. Some tenants will call you names. One tenant, upon being rejected, relieved himself in my hallway. I kid you not, the carpet steamed for ages afterwards. It takes all sorts, his actions only served to remind me of how right I was not to accept him in the first place. I was just sorry I didn't have the CCTV rigged up at the time. I could have made some money from "you've been framed!"

If your application form stated that the tenant's application fee was non-returnable, then it means precisely that. Don't let them upset you, or hassle you; you have done the correct thing, and may have saved your landlord, and yourself untold problems. Put it out of your mind and concentrate on locating a better tenant for the property, as quickly as you can.

If you receive more than one application for a particular property there is nothing to stop you referencing more than one applicant. You can then select the one who you deem to be the best, and keep the second best in reserve, just in case the first choice doesn't complete.

UNEMPLOYED TENANTS:

What do you do if the applicant is not employed? There are two possible scenarios. Firstly the tenant could be paying the rental from private means. For example we had a lady in her late fifties who required a bungalow for a year. We matched her to a very smart little property on the edge of town at £800 per month. She proved she could pay the rent by presenting us with a copy of her bank statement that showed a credit of over a £100,000. We asked her to pay the whole year in advance, which she duly did, £9,600, of which our commission was £960.

As you can imagine, the landlord was delighted to receive a cheque the following week for a full year's rent of £8,640. He had no idea it was coming. You may be surprised how many tenants will pay rental in advance, if you ask for it; there is no harm in asking! It's another weapon in your armoury. If you have a potential tenant who may not be top notch, ask them to pay a goodly proportion of rental up front. They can only say no.

The second possibility is that the potential tenant is unemployed and is expecting the Housing Benefit office to pay all or part of the rental. Housing Benefit is such a wide issue that I have devoted an entire chapter to it a little later in the book. Imagine you have now reached the stage where you have located a good tenant who's passed the referencing procedure with flying colours; you have the landlord's permission to house the tenant in the property. All that remains is for you to prepare the necessary documentation, collect the cash, and book them in. Progress is clearly being made; so let's crack on.

Chapter 11 : Inventories

An Inventory is a list of the contents within a property. With an unfurnished property there may well not be an inventory. Some landlords will prepare one to include items such as light fittings, carpets, kitchen appliances (if supplied) and the like.

As far as any letting agent is concerned, Inventories can be a pain in the neck, because they are so time consuming. The first rule for any agent regarding Inventories is to never promise to produce an Inventory unless it is paid for as an added extra (usually by the landlord). I was stung early in my career when I let a 16 room fully furnished Victorian house. I had previously advertised that I would prepare and check any Inventory for fifty quid. What was I thinking of? The house was crammed from floor to ceiling with eighty years of accrued contents. Never again!

It was furnished from top to bottom right down to and including a packet of cocktail sticks and the landlord took me at my word, and invited me to prepare the inventory. It took me three days! It took all day to check it with the tenant when they moved in, and all day again, when they moved out. By my arithmetic that was five days work for £50, yeeks!

When the tenant moved out there were numerous items missing, but all parties were sure they were there somewhere; it was just that we couldn't find them amid the morass of belongings.

INVENTORIES ARE AN OPPORTUNITY:

So if Inventories are a pain in the neck, and so time consuming, how is it that they are also an opportunity? Why? Because the landlord should pay a realistic additional fee to have them prepared and checked. I will guarantee you now that if you quoted say £200 for the preparation and checking of an Inventory, a reasonable figure for a large house, almost all landlords would forgo the pleasure. Another alternative is for the landlord to prepare an Inventory themselves. Many do, especially on furnished properties. They often have an inflated view of what their sticks and stones are worth. Anyone who has ever invited an auction house around a crammed property will know better what tired old contents are truly worth. Very little, in most cases.

In theory the agent should go through every item, one by one, with the tenant to make sure that everything is present and correct. But the truth is, that many agents, and I am not just talking about the small agencies, but many national agents too, present the Inventory to the tenant and ask them to sign it without a check being made. Most tenants do. It is unsatisfactory, but the landlord has little ground for complaint, after all they are usually most reluctant to pay anything towards the cost of the preparation and checking.

My advice on Inventories would be quite clear. Advise the landlord it is a chargeable extra from the outset. You can put that in your initial fact pack. If they won't accept it, spend as little time on it as you have to. If they are prepared to pay, that's fine, it is another fee for you, to pay for the time that you will undoubtedly have to spend on the chore. Remember, you are a professional person, and you should expect to be paid for your time. There's nothing in this world for free. Never work for nothing.

When the tenant moves out, and the Inventory is checked again, it will no doubt reveal a shortage of a varying degree of items. Most landlords are fair and reasonable, but some are not. Deducting an allowance from the security deposit should in theory pay for the items that are missing or damaged. Occasionally you will come across a landlord who sticks to this to the letter.

For example, one landlord I worked for wanted to claim for a missing yellow pages telephone directory, (they are FREE), half a bar of soap that had long since been used, one dead light bulb, and a used and missing hoover bag! The rental on the property was £1,250 per month and had been paid impeccably. The tenant was foreign. I hate to imagine what impression he took home with him.

Remain cheerful, remain calm, smooth things over, rise above it all and leave. Oh and by the way, the best thing any agent can do to smooth over any ruffles that inventory checks may bring, is to let the property again, as quickly as possible to a fresh tenant, in order to start the rental payments flowing again. Fat rental payments have a knack of making minor disputes evaporate in thin air.

Chapter 12:
Signing Contracts &
Booking Tenants into Property

It goes without saying that the preparation of the legal tenancy agreement is one of the most important duties any letting agent has to accomplish. Quite simply it has to be done right. Errors can be very costly, as we have already seen. Great care should be taken over it, and they should be thoroughly checked, and checked again.

However, once a procedure has been established, providing it is followed rigorously, things improve. It is like so many things, once you have completed one successfully, it is so much easier thereafter.

CHOOSING THE TENANCY AGREEMENT:

There are four likely tenancy agreements that you may consider using. They are:

1. The Oyez printed tenancy agreement from the Law Society
2. A computerised tenancy agreement within purchased or leased software
3. The landlord's own tenancy agreement
4. Your own custom designed agreement

All of these tenancy agreements should be Assured Shorthold Tenancy Agreements. For residential property I highly recommend that you stick with the Assured Shorthold and you won't go far wrong.

The first one, the Oyez, is available from the Law Society and you will need two copies for each let, one is known as the "party" and the other the "counter party". The landlord retains one and the tenant the other.

Note that with Oyez there is a slightly different form for furnished property as opposed to unfurnished. If you are using the Oyez contract, it is a good idea to keep a stock in hand of say 10 of each; readily available in case you need some in a hurry. Incidentally they cost around £2 each.

The benefits of the Oyez contract is that they are spot on, legally speaking, and look the part, but the downside of that contract is that, for many landlords nowadays they are nowhere near comprehensive enough, when it comes to all the do's and don'ts with regard to their precious property.

The second one, the tenancy agreement within a software package is becoming more the norm. The advantages are that you can print off as many as you like, and let as many properties as you wish, and you never need to buy forms as such, although of course the software does need to be purchased or leased. You also never run out. The contract is all embracing running to perhaps six or seven pages with many clauses that the tenant needs to agree to. You can also add additional clauses as some landlords may request, or delete certain clauses if they are obviously incompatible or unacceptable to a particular let. There are not many drawbacks to this type of contract, except perhaps the sheer length of them.

USE A LANDLORD'S AGREEMENT AT YOUR PERIL:

The third tenancy agreement you may have to consider is the landlord's own tenancy agreement. This can be a minefield, and you should tread very warily in that direction. I have seen numerous tenancy agreements prepared by landlords that are frankly not worth the paper they are written on. Some are blatant slightly amended copies of other copyrighted documents, some include clauses that are blatantly illegal, and some are obviously legally flawed. If you prepared a tenancy agreement using a flawed landlord's form, and subsequently there was a problem, the landlord might still have a case against you. His argument could be, "you're the agent, the expert, you should have advised me differently".

I would be very reluctant to use a landlord's own agreement and in all my time as an agent I only ever did so twice. I rejected numerous such agreements as being unacceptable, and most landlords were happy enough to use our agreements once they had inspected them.

To give two examples of what a landlord had included in their own agreements, the first lady had written in that on leaving the property the tenant would return, and at the tenant's expense fully decorate the property from top to bottom.

In my experience that would be unworkable, firstly most tenants would baulk at that to begin with, resulting in lost lets, and secondly I could not imagine any tenant actually carrying out the work, resulting in numerous heated telephone calls, and much wasted time.

Another gentleman had written his own agreement in block capital letters. His spelling was atrocious and it included the clause that the tenant must leave the property at any time during the tenancy within 7 days should the landlord so demand.

This was blatantly illegal, against the terms of an Assured Shorthold Agreement and the Housing Act. I refused point blank to have anything to do with it, and the landlord pressed ahead regardless and installed a tenant who foolishly signed the agreement put before him. The last I heard was that the landlord was being investigated and subsequently prosecuted by the local housing authority for harassing his tenants, and worse.

If you have a landlord who absolutely insists on using his own agreement, ask your solicitor to view it. If the solicitor objected to it in any way, I wouldn't touch it with a barge pole. Find someone else. Move on.

PREPARING YOUR OWN AGREEMENT FORM:

The last choice would be an agreement you may be tempted to prepare from scratch yourself. The advantages of this would be that you could include whatever clauses you think were appropriate, and you would never have to pay a penny for it. However the great disadvantage is that you run the very real risk that you could produce a document that is not legally binding.

It may look OK to you, but are you legally qualified to know? Did you know for example that the size of margins on an agreement is supposed to be of a certain dimension? On that technicality alone, a judge could set aside an agreement, in the case of a dispute.

How would you care to ring a landlord and explain that you couldn't get a tenant out of their property, because the agreement you had produced, had been set aside by a judge as being illegal. It doesn't bear thinking about does it? If you're tempted to set up your own contract, and I can see that after you gain experience, you might be, you absolutely must have it inspected and passed by a solicitor. And don't forget that you must not copy, word for word, other agreements that you may have come across. They are invariably copyrighted, and you would be committing an offence if you did so. The penalties for breaching copyright are rightly harsh. Don't take the risk.

It sounds heavy I know, but you can appreciate that a legally binding contract simply has to be prepared absolutely correctly. To muck around with something you do not truly understand, could be a recipe for disaster. I used the Oyez contracts for many years, before switching to a computerised product within a software package. I can honestly say that in all that time during which we prepared thousands of agreements, we never had a serious problem with regard to an incorrectly completed agreement.

My advice would be, once you have prepared your first agreement, have your solicitor cast their eye over it before it is presented to the landlord or tenant for their signature. Once you've completed one successfully, you will rapidly gain confidence in preparing countless others thereafter.

So you've sorted out your contracts and prepared them, and it's now time to look at the occasionally fractious business of tenant's deposits.

TENANT'S DEPOSITS:

Almost all landlords require a security deposit to be paid along with the first month's rental. This deposit is more often than not the equivalent of an additional month's rent. Some agents and some landlords are nowadays seeking more than one month's rent as a deposit, perhaps a month and a half, or a month plus £150, or even two months. You can ask for any amount of security deposit you wish, but do remember that once you ask for more than a month's rent as a deposit you will dramatically reduce the number of applications you will receive for any particular property.

Many tenants will baulk at paying more than a month. Take a detached house for example that could be on your books for £850 per month. If the tenant needed to pay £850 first month's rent, plus another £850 deposit, plus your processing fee of say £100, they would need to find £1,800 in cash before they could contemplate moving in. For many people that is a hefty sum. But if you then increased the deposit to say a month and half, that same tenant would need to find a whopping £2,225.

There are many people out there with that kind of money readily available, but equally there are many well-qualified employed people who don't have that kind of ready cash. Does the landlord really want to pass up on an otherwise excellent tenant in full time employment because they can't or won't stump up an additional deposit? In my experience most landlords would prefer to have the house let. So would I, every time.

To some extent you need to liase with the landlord, some will tell you their terms with regard to deposits and will never budge; others will take your advice. If it was my house and it was empty, and the tenant had passed all their references and was paying a full month's deposit I would always accept them.

An empty property is a liability, and it could be another three months before you locate someone else who was prepared to pay that extra deposit. If it stayed empty for three months that would be a loss of rental on that property of £2,550, a loss that could never be recovered no matter how soon it was let, and all because of a small additional deposit. You have to be realistic.

What happens to the deposit? If you are managing the property, you must retain the deposit yourself in the client's bank account. Do NOT pass it to the landlord, as you will be responsible for returning it to the tenant at the end of the agreement. If you give it to the landlord and he disappears or goes bust, you would still have to refund it out of your own pocket.

Some unscrupulous landlords may hassle you for it, but you must resist them. Remember, it is not the landlord's money, it belongs to the tenant and they have handed it over to you for safekeeping.

If you are not managing the property, but merely finding a tenant for the landlord, you will need to pass the deposit to the landlord with his first payment, but make sure that this is clearly stated in your documentation and that the tenant understands, and agrees, that this is where his deposit is going. That way he will have no come back on you at a later date should a dispute of any kind between the two parties rear its head. The managing of deposits is covered in more detail in the Accounting chapter.

FINALISING CONTRACTS:

Your contracts are ready to be signed. It makes no difference whether the landlord or the tenant signs first. If you have a quiet afternoon pop round and see the landlord and get him to sign. Don't be tempted to send contracts through the post if you can avoid it. Never send contracts to tenants through the post. If you did, you would have no idea who had actually signed the agreement. Once the landlord has signed they can't change their mind, or rent the property to someone else, or give it to another agent, all good reasons to have them sign as quickly as possible.

You should already have made it clear to the tenant that you must have CLEARED funds before you would be able to release the keys. In other words if the tenant is meeting you to sign at the house, and pay on the day the contract is due to start, the tenant must pay in cash, or by banker's draft, for ALL the monies due.

DO NOT accept under any circumstances at this late stage a personal cheque for either the rental OR the deposit. If the tenant does not pay with cleared funds, DO NOT RELEASE THE KEY. Sob stories about having nowhere else to sleep are irrelevant. The tenant clearly knew that cleared funds were required. It should say so on your application form. If they can't, or won't produce the cash, it may mean their personal cheque will bounce.

One way of avoiding last minute hassle is to arrange to meet the tenant a week or more before the contract starts either at your office, the tenant's existing house, or at the property they are renting, but do make absolutely sure that you allow enough time for personal cheques to clear.

Banks take longer than you think to clear personal cheques. Don't believe the three-day rubbish they trot out. It's a fallacy. And if you express clear a personal cheque, remember there is a charge. The tenant should pay it. Why should you? It would be disastrous as I am sure you can imagine to receive a letter from the bank a day or two <u>after</u> the tenant has moved into a property, stating that their cheque had bounced.

If in doubt, RING YOUR BANK
If in doubt, DON'T RELEASE KEYS
UNTIL YOU KNOW for CERTAIN
That ALL funds have cleared.

ARRANGE ONGOING PAYMENTS:

You will need to give the tenant a receipt for all monies received. If you are NOT managing the property it is yet another opportunity to remind them that the landlord will be holding the deposit, and that if the tenant has any maintenance problems they should contact the landlord direct, and not pester you.

If you are managing the property on an ongoing basis you will need to make arrangements to collect future rental, and far and away the best method of doing this, is by standing order mandate. You can obtain a typical standing order mandate from your bank, or you can design your own on your PC. Suggest to ALL tenants they pay by standing order mandate. Some agents insist on payment by SOM and will not entertain tenants unless they agree. If they are reluctant to agree, you might ask yourself why?

If a tenant says, I'm not paying by Direct Debit because you might take whatever you like from my account, take the opportunity to politely correct them. A standing order mandate is NOT the same thing as a direct debit. A standing order mandate is always in the control of the account holder, the tenant, unlike a direct debit. Only the account holder can start and stop standing order payments, and only they can amend the amounts paid.

If the tenancy started on the 15th of October and they have paid the first month's rent up front along with the deposit, the next rental payment is obviously due on November 15th. The standing order therefore should state "please pay £500 (or whatever the figure is) on the fifteen of November to Brent's Rents and on the fifteenth of each month thereafter until cancelled by me".

Once you have the tenant's signature on the SOM take a photocopy of it for your records, and then mail or deliver by hand, the original by first class post to the tenant's bank. Put a note in your diary when the next payment is due to appear and check the bank account daily to see what payments are in, and more importantly, what payments are not.

SETUP UP ONLINE BANKING:

I strongly advise you to have a computerised online bank statement facility with your bank. That way you can check two or three times a day, if need be, from your own office, and it saves having to ring the bank when you will almost certainly be put on hold more often as not. I don't know about you but those PRESS 3 type of automated answering machines are one of the banes of my life! As for eventually getting through to someone on the other side of the planet who can barely speak English, well that type of dreadful service beggar's belief.

If the tenant will not agree to a standing order mandate being set up, perhaps it is because there is no money in their bank account, in which case another warning light should start flashing. One way of insisting a tenant pays by standing order, is to state as much, before the let is finally agreed.

You do not need to make a big issue of it; you can simply say, the landlord requires the rent to be paid by standing order mandate directly to us. If they don't agree, why don't they? In my experience good tenants always agree. They don't want to have to bother writing out and posting off cheques every month, anymore than you do.

AVOID HAVING TO COLLECT RENTS IN PERSON:

Nevertheless, despite your best efforts, some tenants, even if they agree to pay by SOM initially, will not do so for long. The alternatives are for them to drop cheques and or cash into your office, but whatever you do, don't be railroaded into chasing them round collecting the rent. That is not your responsibility. It is the tenant's responsibility to deliver the rent to your office or to your bank account. Chasing after people is a massive time waster.

Avoid it wherever you can. Retain the initiative and put the onus on them to deliver. If the tenant smells a weakness in your resolve, they may well start playing games with you. "Can you come and collect it at 7pm?" You go in the rain, and they're not in. They think it's funny, you won't, and neither will the landlord. If there were more than one incidence of that, I would write them a straight letter reminding them of their responsibilities.

BOOKING TENANTS IN:

Once the tenant has paid all the upfront money and the funds are cleared, and once both parties have signed the agreement, you can release their copy of the tenancy agreement, and arrange to book them into the property. The landlord's copy can be sent to him or her, together with their first statement of account and payment.

When you book the tenant into the property you MUST always attend. Never give the key to the tenant in your office and wish them luck. ALWAYS arrange to meet them at the property. While you are there with the tenant make a note of the gas and electricity meter readings and have the tenant sign your booking in slip to confirm the figures. The tenant should also sign for the quantity of keys you are issuing.

Go round the property with the tenant and make a note of any obvious damage or noticeable wear and tear at the property. For example the lounge carpet may be badly stained. Note the fact. Photograph it too, if you think it will show up. Perhaps a small pane in the glazed front door may be cracked, again note the fact on your file. The reason

109

for noting imperfections such as this is because at the end of the contract, if the landlord attempts to make a claim against the deposit, you can refer to your notes, and photographs, and say "sorry but that was like that before the tenant moved in".

Take the opportunity to have the tenant sign the Inventory too, if one is supplied or has been prepared by you or the landlord. It should be in duplicate in order that the tenant can keep one copy, and you can retain the other. The Inventory can and often is attached to the tenancy agreement, and forms part of the contract.

In my experience no matter how many things you may check in the property on the day the tenancy starts, it is quite impossible to categorically say whether everything in the house is working perfectly or not. It is not until someone actually moves into a house that minor problems might appear. For example you wouldn't know if the central heating started banging loudly after it has been on for twenty minutes, or that the immersion heater cuts out after ten.

Thus I always said to every tenant, "if there's anything else that shows up in the next day or so please let us know". That way you can list any defects on the file and report them to the landlord. You won't hear a word from most tenants again, while some, at the opposite end of the spectrum, will pester you with a huge list of the most minor defects. There is nothing wrong with that, at least you know about it, it's on the record.

You've read the meters, and don't forget the water meter if there is one, you've checked the property over, the tenant has signed and paid, and has been issued with his copy of the agreement. There only remain a couple of little things to do before you can get away. It's always a very good idea to ask the tenant to go outside, close the front door, and re-enter the property using the keys you have just issued. This not only ensures the keys are the right ones, but with so many unusual locks around these days, it saves you the possibility of having to return at a later hour to demonstrate how to lock and unlock doors. It happens believe me, and quite a lot. Tilt and slide conservatory doors can be a real nuisance in this respect.

Finally you can expect the tenant to ask you, especially if it is winter, to show them how to use the central heating. This can be a pain too, as many systems differ. If they ask you to demonstrate, it's very difficult to refuse, so a little earlier practice may well pay dividends. And it will check that the heating is actually working.

REPORT THE METER READINGS:

When you have finished your tasks at the property, return to the office and write to the utility companies. (Gas, Water, Electric, and Council Tax). Advise them that Mister Karpov moved into 50 Pretty Villas, Halton, on the 15th of May. Give them the meter readings if you have them. The reason for these letters is that once you've advised the service suppliers of a new tenant being installed, all new bills will then automatically be sent directly to the tenant. Your landlord, or yourself, if the house belongs to you, are then clear of any responsibility for those services.

Even if the absolute worst came to the worst and the tenant never paid a penny to any of the utility companies, they cannot then turn to you, or the property owner, and say, "it's your house, you pay the £1,000 electricity bill", providing:

a)   a proper tenancy agreement was in force, and
b)   you have written to them and advised them that the tenant was now in residence.

If there were no legitimate tenancy agreement in existence the owner of the house could still be responsible for all bills.

Lastly you might like to ring the landlord, for public relations purposes, and say: "the tenant's now booked into the house, everything went well, and you'll receive a payment in 7 days", or whatever you have previously agreed. It also gives you the opportunity to mention, "oh by the way there is a loose slate or two at the front", or anything else that came up during your visit.

Be upbeat about it, you should be, for you have successfully let the property in the face of fierce competition from all the other companies that traipse over your beat. They didn't do it, you did! Be brave and ask the landlord "have you anything else to rent? I've another really nice person looking". They'll soon tell you if they have, and they'll remember you too, if another of their houses suddenly becomes empty. There will be times when you have to ring landlords with bad news, so make the most of it when you are calling them with good.

Set up Standing Order Mandates
Arrange on line banking facilities
Note meter readings
Write to the Utility companies
Arrange for tenants to sign inventories
Note and photograph property imperfections

Chapter 13 : Statements & Accounting

When you start your property management business you should make sure you open two distinct and quite separate business bank accounts, namely:

1. Your Current Account: this contains YOUR money paying YOUR bills

2. Client's Account: this contains the client's rental and deposit monies, and does NOT belong to you

Start as you mean to go on. These two accounts are entirely separate and should NEVER be confused or intermingled. NEVER pay any of your bills from the client's account. This would be tantamount to stealing. You would be using other people's cash for your own purposes.

At the time of writing there is no regulation dealing with Letting Agents handling client's deposits but this is an issue the government is constantly reviewing. It is quite possible that legislation introducing regulation will be introduced in the near future. The first thing the regulators could check, once they had the powers to do so, would be accounting practices, especially with a view to the balances in client's accounts.

Woe betide any agent or landlord who experienced a spot check, and was found to have dipped into, or muddled up the client's money, or worse still, had spent it. It happens. Prosecution would unquestionably follow. Be warned. Client's money is precisely that. Abuse it at your peril.

Get it right from the start, keep it right, and have it rigorously audited by an independent auditor or accountant at least once a year. If you adhere to these simple rules you won't go far wrong, and you shouldn't have a problem.

When you receive the rental payments, ALL rental payments and tenant's deposits should be banked directly into the Client's account using the appropriate pay in book or directed there by standing order mandate. Thus all your mandate forms should bear only the client's account bank details.

BANK ALL MONIES QUICKLY:

Always bank money as quickly as you can. Try not to leave money unbanked overnight, and never leave cash and cheques lying around in the house or office where an opportunistic sneak thief might stumble on it. Bank every day.

Remember, if you received a thousand pounds rent and a thousand pounds deposit from a tenant, and then lost it, you would have to make it good out of your own pocket (notwithstanding any insurance policies that might assist you). This would be an expensive but very easy mistake to make.

Make sure that the client's account is interest bearing. If in doubt, ask your bank manager to confirm. You will be pleasantly surprised how quickly the balance of this account will rise. For example if you had fifty tenants paying an average £700 deposit the balance in that account would be £35,000. By the time the monthly rental payments had flooded in as well, you could double that figure, and it's all accruing interest.

If you had a hundred properties, as many agencies do, even the smaller ones, you could double that figure again. If you had a thousand properties, well you get the picture. So you can see the client's account bank balance could reach huge figures, and the great thing is, neither the landlord nor the tenant, is entitled to any interest on that money. The interest belongs to you, the agent, and quite rightly so. After all it is you who have to pay all the bank charges on that account, and it is you who is providing the service of keeping the money safe and sound, albeit in your local high street bank.

Your bank manager will think you are wonderful, and it won't be long before he's inviting you to dinner, mark my words they do, and doesn't that make a pleasant change to the usual calls bank managers make? In times of low interest rates the interest accrued is nothing special. But in times of high interest levels, you will be very pleased to see your quarterly bank statement, and you have just created another income stream, a stream that requires almost no work, and is very reliable.

PREPARING LANDLORDS STATEMENTS:

Once you have banked the cash, you should prepare the landlord's statement. Different software packages produce differing styles of invoices, but they should show the following basic details:

- Landlord's name and address. Include the full address with postcode, so you can use window envelopes. They save a great deal of time addressing letters
- The tenant's name
- The date and amount of rental collected
- The deposit (if you are not managing the property and transferring it over)
- A separate note of the deposit received if you are managing the property, but remember NOT to include it in the arithmetical calculation

- Any deductions, such as insurance premiums, repairs that you may have organised, or inventory compilation
- Your fees and commission, which should be deducted from the gross amount received

So as an example imagine you have let a flat at £500.00 pcm, and you are managing the property. Your standard fee is £100 on each let plus 10% of the collected rental. There were no insurance deductions or repairs. The arithmetic would look like this.

Deposit received and retained 500.00

Rent received		500.00
Landlords Fee	100.00	
10% commission	50.00	
Total deductions		150.00
Balance Due to Landlord		£350.00

There is no VAT shown because you are not yet VAT registered. If you were, your fees would be liable for VAT too, currently at a rate of 17.5%. VAT is not currently chargeable on residential rentals

PREPARING THE LANDLORD'S PAYMENT:

A payment may then be prepared from the client's account for the landlord. There are two recommended methods of paying landlords, by cheque or direct bank transfer. Never get involved in dishing out cash to landlords, not only is it a security risk, it is most unprofessional. And if you do it once, I guarantee the landlord will be forever hovering around outside your office, waiting for their next whack of cash. Don't go there.

I greatly favour the direct bank transfer payment method for four good reasons.

1. It is much cheaper as far as bank charges are concerned
2. The cheques cannot be lost in the post or mislaid

3. The money hits the landlord's account quickly and efficiently and is easily trackable and traceable

4. There is less clerical work involved

In saying that, there are still many landlords who prefer to see a cheque accompanying their monthly statement, and that is their prerogative.

Never become involved with using the landlord's money, at the landlord's request, to pay a third party not known to you, or paying their mortgage direct. That could cause fearful problems. For example they may notice at a later date when their accounts were being audited, that they did not receive a payment in March, but they may forget that you paid someone else at their request. You might forget too, and pay the landlord, in effect for a second time. Always pay the landlord's money, to the landlord.

If you agreed to pay their mortgage directly and for some reason a payment went missing, imagine the landlord's fury if they received a written warning letter from the building society or bank, possibly even threatening re-possession. It's a potential pitfall you want nothing to do with.

Save the statement on your computer, and when the next month's payment comes round, you can simply adjust the dates, saving a lot of work again. Don't forget though to remove the £100 fee, as that was a one off, so the next month's balance to the landlord, on that let, assuming no additional deductions, would be £450.

Where you are not managing a property, and the pre agreed fee is half a month's rental, your arithmetic would look like this.

Deposit received	500.00
Rent received	500.00
Landlords Fee	250.00-
Balance due to Landlord £750.00	

This time because you are not managing the property the deposit is included, and is being paid over to the landlord. If the landlord had instructed you to set up an insurance policy or do any other work, such as a gas safety check, now is the time to make sure the cost is deducted, because unlike a full management contract, you will have no further funds to deduct the expenses from in the future. Print out hard copies for yourself as a permanent record, and save all statements on your computer.

Once the statement of account is finalised you can proceed to preparing and authorising the payment, again from the client's account.

TOTALLING YOUR OWN FEES:

At the end of each month you can tot up the total fees charged to your landlords. These fees are now your money. Imagine you had twenty-three accounts, seventeen of which produced £60 fees, three producing £275, and three producing £250, your total fees billed for that month would be £2,595.

That is:

$$17 \times 60 = 1020$$
$$3 \times 275 = 825$$
$$3 \times 250 = 750$$
Total £2,595

This figure should then be transferred from the client's account, to your business's current account, on the first day of the month. A summary justifying the payment should be prepared and kept on file.

If there has been any interest received, (interest is usually credited quarterly and tax is deducted before the money is paid to you by your bank), then you can add that to the summary too. One month in three there should be interest for you, and that can be transferred out of the client's account at the same time.

If you have any doubts about whether you are dealing correctly with the payments and transfers from the client's account do not hesitate to discuss it with your accountant. He will immediately set you right if you are making mistakes. Remember, it is far better to put mistakes right in the first month, rather than at a later date. Monthly mistakes carried over can mount up very quickly, and you don't want to be facing a refund back to the client's account.

One final point, if you buy or lease specialised property computer software to look after your statements, it will do most of this for you, including all the arithmetical calculations. If you want my advice, get some. It will give your business a more professional image, cachet if you prefer, and your systems will forever be updated as times and procedures inevitably evolve.

Open the correct bank accounts
Never leave money lying about
Bank Money Quickly
Prepare landlord's statements
Action landlord payments
Prepare monthly summary of fees earned
Pay yourself the balance of the summary

Chapter 14 : The Riddle that is Housing Benefit

There is no topic or aspect of property letting and management that is guaranteed to stir up the blood as much as the riddle that is Housing Benefit. It doesn't matter whether you are renting three or four properties of your own, or are managing six hundred properties, as a successful property agency, the subject of Housing Benefit will rear its head.

You have two stark choices, you either become an expert on it, or you ignore it, that's for you to decide. For my part I will try and put across the benefits (sorry to use that word again) and problems that this animal can produce.

It's true there are more myths and legends about Housing Benefit than just about anything else in the property world. I'm sure you will have heard of many of them before. Something along these lines:

1. Housing Benefit is guaranteed
2. The Agent collects the Benefit direct, the tenant can't then redirect it
3. Housing Benefit cannot be reclaimed by the Benefit office
4. Housing Benefit will pay all the contracted rental
5. Housing Benefit will come through straight away
6. Housing Benefit office is easy to deal with
7. Everyone is entitled to Housing Benefit
8. The Letting Agent is responsible for sorting out the Benefit

9. The Housing Benefit will automatically increase every year
10. Housing Benefit is easy

Ladies and gentlemen I am sure you won't be surprised to learn that ALL of those statements are incorrect, and yet they are often trotted out, and many more besides. They sometimes lead to the ready-made excuses that some Housing Benefit tenants dream up, such as:

1. I can't pay the rent this month because the Benefit's not come through, or
2. I can't pay the rent this month because the giro's lost in the post and even:
3. I can't pay the rent because the Benefit Office is on strike.

Where do you start and why bother? Well perhaps surprisingly there are good reasons to bother, so let's start at the top and look at those ten initial statements.

HOUSING BENEFIT IS GUARANTEED

It is NOT. It never has been and never will be. Each person is assessed for Housing Benefit on their individual merits. Some qualify, some don't.

THE AGENT COLLECTS THE BENEFIT DIRECT

Many agents do collect benefit directly into their clients bank account, and there are good and bad reasons for doing so, but a tenant can at any time go into the Benefit office and redirect those benefits back to themselves with one simple letter. It is THEIR benefit, and although they sign a letter stating that it will be spent on rental payments ONLY, in many cases, that is simply not true.

PAID BENEFIT CANNOT BE RECLAIMED

Nonsense. Oh yes it can! A friend of mine, an elderly landlady had a tenant in a property for three years and in all that time the Benefit office paid the entire rental totalling just over £9,000. The tenant then disappeared and the following month, the landlady received a letter from the Council requesting that ALL that money be returned, as the tenant had claimed it illegally. The landlady is still fighting the case through the courts, and I wish her well.

HOUSING BENEFIT WILL PAY ALL THE RENT

Rubbish! They have restrictions and guidelines to decide how much they may contribute. They might pay it all, they might not, in fact they might not pay any of it.

HOUSING BENEFIT COMES THROUGH STRAIGHT AWAY

Oh, I wish! In one fairly recent case it took Liverpool City Council seven months before payments commenced. I'm sure they would say differently, but it seemed to me they were deliberately obstructing payments at every turn. They couldn't possibly have been doing that, could they?

THE HOUSING BENEFIT OFFICE IS EASY TO DEAL WITH

Some are better than others. I sympathise with anyone who works on the front desk in any Housing Benefit office. They are rushed off their feet, tempers fray, and verbal abuse is a common occurrence. Physical abuse isn't unheard of either. I'd want a premier league footballers pay to take that job. You won't be surprised to learn that the staff doesn't appear to hang around too long.

EVERYONE IS ENTITLED TO HOUSING BENEFIT

Once again that is gibberish! I'm not for a start, and I doubt if you are either.

THE LETTING AGENT IS RESPONSIBLE FOR SORTING OUT THE HB

What a laugh! They certainly are NOT! Some lazy tenants may tell you that. You tell them to get of their backsides and go and get the matter sorted. It is THEIR benefit and it is THEIR responsibility to sort it out.

HOUSING BENEFIT AUTOMATICALLY INCREASES

Nope is doesn't. You can apply for an increase annually, but there is no certainty you will receive anything. In one recent case the increase my most successful landlord received was 12 pence! It didn't even pay for the stamp on the application.

So after that litany you might be forgiven for asking again, why bother? The fact is, that at some point in our lives we can all lose our jobs, we can all be between jobs, and most of us in those circumstances, would turn to the benefit office to assist paying our rent.

If as an agent we stated right at the outset that we would only take tenants in full time employment, that's fine, but there is nothing to say an existing employed tenant might not be made redundant, two month's down the line. If that happened, the chances are, you would have a tenant on your books on Housing Benefit, regardless of your up front restrictions. What are you going to do then?

Being in receipt of HB is not grounds for evicting someone. Whether you like it or not, it might be better to know how the system works.

TENANTS ON BENEFIT:

Here are some specific examples of tenants of mine who were in receipt of HB. In my last year as a property manager I had a former Nat West bank manager who'd recently been made redundant, an unemployed solicitor who looked over a few things of mine when he had nothing better to do, and a lecturer from Bristol University between posts, and they were all on Housing Benefit. Were they bad tenants? Of course not! They were in fact excellent tenants in every other respect. So why not entertain tenants such as these in the first place?

The fact is there are some people on Housing Benefit you might consider and some you wouldn't, just the same as employed people. If you rejected them all out of hand because they were on benefit, you would be harming your own business, because you would be missing that business. I suggest you at least consider Housing Benefit cases, no more, no less, consider every case carefully on its merits.

What sort of tenants wouldn't I take? I had four lads aged eighteen and nineteen none of whom were working. I didn't consider housing them, would you have? They might have been really nice kids, but they could go and live somewhere else as far as I was concerned. I go back the Me-Me-Me test. Would I consider placing these guys unsupervised in my own house? If the answer was no, that would be the end of it as far as I was concerned. The answer was no!

I respect your views if your decide against any benefit cases in any circumstances, and I'm sure you will run a successful business regardless, it's just that it won't expand as rapidly as it might otherwise. And let's face it; we are in the property business to make money. We want to grow as quickly as we can. And I'll tell you another thing, some landlords LIKE housing benefit tenants. I kid you not. This applies especially in the poorer areas, and I'm using the word 'poorer' in connection with the housing stock.

In areas of poor quality housing, landlords often look upon Housing Benefit as kindly as the tenants do, they rely on it, the fact is they would be in trouble without it. They don't want to see the system changed too much, or worse still, abolished, as some people would like.

So now, I suppose, you want me to tell you precisely how the Housing Benefit Scheme works in your area, and I'd tell you, except the system varies from one local authority to another. Standardisation has yet to hit the HB market. Perhaps one day it will, but it isn't here yet. Nevertheless this will give you a general idea:

HOUSING BENEFIT GENERAL GUIDELINES:

Housing Benefit, and from now one I'm going to refer to is as HB is assessed on a weekly basis. Each person is assessed separately, based on their individual circumstances, so even if you owned four identical houses in a row, all rented out to four tenants in receipt of HB, it is quite feasible you would receive four different payments.

Once the applicant has lodged his or her claim with the HB office, and I'll return to their claim forms in a minute or two, in some areas a low interim payment is sanctioned quite quickly. Perhaps £35 a week when in fact the property may well be assessed at £80 pw.

The claim form then drops onto an almighty pile of similar claims that are then waded through by the hard-pressed HB staff. I am convinced that the tenants and agents who enquire of the progress of these claims most often, who ring, nay pester, the HB office, are the ones whose claims are sorted the quickest. I am sure the HB office would deny this, and won't thank me for saying so, but I speak as I find. In other words if you have a lazy tenant who couldn't give a fig whether the paperwork is processed or not, you will almost certainly be kept waiting a lot longer before your payments begin to flow.

The rent officer inspects the claim and he will then assess the final payment the benefit office will make. In many cases he will need to visit the tenant in the property. He might check out the standard of the house or flat, he might have additional questions for the tenant, perhaps regarding a previous benefit claim. But they don't visit the house every time. It may be that there's been a benefit tenant in that house or a very similar property before. The rent officer may know the house. It may be that the tenant has claimed before, and in these circumstances the assessing officer may make his decision without ever moving from his desk.

When they have decided what benefit is to be paid, they will write to the tenant and advise them of the figure. They will also write to the agent, if there is one, providing the tenant has ticked a particular box on their application form authorising them so to do.

There is no definitive time that you can rely on between lodging the claim and receiving the first cash payment from the benefit office, but 5 weeks would be a fair guess, 10 weeks not unheard of. It depends on how much of a backlog there is your area, and how much of a sense of urgency your tenant possesses. Not to mention how straight they are. A backlog of some proportion is the one thing you can rely on.

KEEPING LANDLORDS INFORMED KEEPS LANDLORDS HAPPY:

If there is going to be a delay in rent flowing, and there almost certainly will be, the landlord would need to be made aware that payments would not start until the assessment process had been completed. In other words a landlord housing a tenant in receipt of benefit may have to wait up to three months before he could receive any payment, unless the tenant could be persuaded to make rental payments upfront in the intervening period. Always assuming they were capable, and agreeable, to doing so.

When that happens the tenant would need to be reimbursed for any credit balance on their rent account once the housing benefit payments kicked in. In my experience most tenants will be hassling you for the refund the moment it is due. That is their right of course.

The payments are almost always backdated to the date of the claim, which should coincide with the start date of the tenancy agreement. In most geographical areas, but not all, payments are made in four-weekly tranches. Thus if a tenant were finally assessed at £75 per week the payment on the Schedule would be £300 for that tenant for a four weekly period. The dates that the payment covered are listed on the Schedule supplied by the benefit office, so you can keep an accurate track of which weeks you have been paid for.

HOW ARE BENEFIT PAYMENTS MADE?

How is the payment made, and to whom? When the tenant fills out their application form, they need to fill in various boxes that relate to payment. They can decide to have the payment sent directly to themselves, either directly into their bank account, or more usually via a giro cheque through the mail to the tenant's address.

In theory the tenant should then draw the money and hand it to the landlord, or landlord's agent to pay the rent. The tenant could get into trouble if they use the money for any other purpose. But of course it doesn't stop them sometimes doing so. If you had four screaming hungry kids and £300 in your hand, you might be tempted to spend some of it, if not all, in the local supermarket, (how many of us would do the same thing given the same circumstances?) If this happens, the rent could remain unpaid, at the very least, in part.

However, the tenant has another option, in that they can sign over their benefit to be paid directly to the landlord, or landlord's agent, and the majority nowadays do this. It gives them a fairly hassle free life. They can sit back and believe the government is paying their rental direct, and they have nothing to worry about. And it is true that once payments have been set up and start flowing, they can run on uninterrupted for twelve months, or more in some cases, before the HB office will look at the situation again.

BENEFIT   CONTRIBUTIONS   VERSUS
CONTRACTED RENTAL:

Imagine a situation where a tenant has passed all his references, and paid the necessary deposit. They sign a contract at £400 per month. They are in receipt of benefit and the final assessment is notified to be £85.72 per week. (Yes the figures can be as odd as that). What happens then?

If the agent, or landlord, receives £85.72 per week in four weekly slugs, the agent would receive £342.88 every four weeks. But there are thirteen 'four weekly' periods in a year so in effect the agent would receive £342.88 x 13 = £4457.44 per annum. Therefore on a calendar monthly basis the agent is receiving from the HB the equivalent of £371.45 per calendar month. (That's the £4,457.44 divided by 12).

Still with that? I know it seems unnecessarily complicated but you need to understand the arithmetic for one very good reason. It is clear that the HB are not, in this case, covering the rental in full, so the agent would need to approach the tenant and ask for the shortfall to be made up. The shortfall figure in this case, being £28.55 per month.

MAKING UP SHORTFALL FIGURES:

The best way to obtain shortfalls once the figure is known, is to ask the tenant to make a payment by standing order to keep the rent account up to date. This also ensures that the account doesn't slip into arrears in the future. If it does slip into arrears over a period of time, it is very difficult to bring matters into line later.

Some tenants in poorer property do not even have a bank account, and clearly they would not be able to pay any shortfall by SOM. You would have to ask them to call into the office and make up the shortfall in person. The shortfall figure could be larger or smaller than the figure shown here. If you are not too busy you might consider collecting it yourself from the tenant, but I would not recommend you start doing that. You'd be setting a dangerous precedent and before long they would expect you to collect it.

Imagine if you had 25 similar tenants all making up small shortfalls, and you trying to collect them all on the doorstep. Half the time the door wouldn't be opened and you'd have to return later. Imagine the time you would waste chasing around smallish amounts of cash. You won't need me to tell you that would be terrible time management. The answer is to insist that tenants pay by standing order, or send you a cheque, or deliver cash to you in person.

Alternatively some tenants ask their parents to pay the shortfall by standing order and many do. You could even suggest that idea to tenants faced with a shortfall figure. As Sven might say, why not? It works, and any system that produces rental payments should be considered.

ESTABLISH A SYSTEM AT THE OUTSET:

At the beginning of the let, find out if the tenant is intending to claim HB. You'll have a very good hint if there is no employer listed on the application form. If the answer is "yes" you should discuss with them to whom the benefit is to be paid. Do this at the earliest opportunity. Never leave it until the tenant is in the property. Remember, before the tenant signs the agreement and takes they keys, you hold all the cards, afterwards you don't.

If the tenant is intending to apply for HB insist they complete the benefit forms and lodge them at the HB office immediately. You might even consider taking the tenant to the benefit office yourself, that way you would know for certain they had indeed been there. A colleague of mine did that, and it worked very well. You could even mention to the landlord, "Yes Mister Johnson, I know they have been to the HB office because I took them there myself!"

Your landlord will be impressed by your keenness if nothing else. This is something that large agencies would never consider doing in a million years. But who cares what they do? You will run your business as you see fit, and anything that speeds up rent should be considered.

Don't forget to remind the tenant to ask the HB for a receipt for all documents lodged, as they are notorious for losing things. At a later date if they are shown a valid receipt, they will make more of an effort to trace the paperwork. They will know for a fact they have actually had the documents, as opposed to a tenant telling them porky-pies. (Yes that does happen sometimes, unfortunately, you won't be surprised to know).

PROS & CONS OF DIRECT PAYMENTS:

There are BIG pros and cons regarding collecting benefit directly.

PROS:

1. The money comes to you and the tenant doesn't see it, and thus can't spend it
2. You can monitor clearly what is coming in and make arrangements to collect the shortfall, if any
3. You are immediately aware of any change in the scale of payments and can take action accordingly

CONS:

1. There is one huge downside of receiving benefit payments direct, and this is it. You receive rental payments from the benefit office for a particular tenant in good faith, and duly pay it over to the landlord, less your commission. If at a later date the HB office decide in their wisdom, they have overpaid you, or made a mistake in making a payment in the first place, the HB will come back to you for a partial, or in the worst case scenario, a full refund of all the monies paid to you. Worse still they might even deduct it from a future payment

Schedule without giving you the opportunity to dispute their decision.

Not nice. So what can you do about that?

HOUSING BENEFIT OFFICE RECLAIMING PAYMENTS:

Imagine if you had <u>incorrectly</u> received monies on behalf of a tenant of £95 per week for a year. You would have received £4,940 in total, and that is the figure the HB might ask you to pay back. Why might the HB office change their minds and ask for benefit back? There are several possible reasons. Perhaps the tenant lied on their application form, perhaps they were in full time employment all along, and were not entitled to housing benefit at all. Regrettably that happens sometimes.

Your obvious next course of action would be to ask the landlord to reimburse you. Do you think you'd get it? You might, but for a start the landlord might have gone abroad. Secondly he might not have any money. And thirdly he might say to you, "you're the agent you should have managed it better". If you took the landlord to court, you'd probably win, but that's messy and unproductive, and time consuming, and who wants to gain a reputation for suing their own clients?

The answer is, to vet your tenants very carefully from day one. If you have any doubts about them, any gut feeling that everything is not quite as it should be, bin the application! Never turn a blind eye to dodgy housing benefit claims, for they will surely come back to haunt you big time at a later date.

ASSESSING BENEFIT APPLICANTS:

Here are some further tips that might help you in your assessing procedure:

The prospective tenant says, "oh yeah, my fella will be living with us, but I don't want him to be on the tenancy agreement, it helps with the benefit, you know what I mean?"

Answer: NO! If the chap is going to be living in the house, his name must be on the tenancy agreement. Why wouldn't it be? The HB will want to see the tenancy agreement and the benefit will be assessed accordingly. In this case the bloke is quite likely to be employed. What they are proposing is illegal, and a blatant attempt to defraud the HB office. Remember HB is ultimately paid for by all of us, the taxpayers, and fraud could never be encouraged.

The prospective tenant says, "I've been working abroad so I can't give you a landlords or credit reference".

Answer: It's amazing how many people who want to claim benefit have suddenly returned from abroad. (It might be true, but just as likely it could be a fib, and they could be hiding from their appalling track record of previous poor payment.) Ask them to produce proof of earnings whilst working abroad, and ask them for an employer's reference anyway. There's nothing to stop you emailing a company in Nova Scotia, or wherever else, for a reference. The world's a small place these days.

But it can be difficult to credit reference someone who's been living in Wagga Wagga or Swaziland, and clued-up tenants know this. I'd be very suspicious of any application hiding behind the, "we've been working abroad" excuse unless they could produce full documentary history of their recent employment record. Demand a first class guarantor anyway. No guarantor, then bin it.

Then there's the prospective tenant who says, "you can have all the benefit, but I won't be able to make up any shortfall".

Answer: The shortfall might be three quarters of the total rental. No shortfall payments, no tenancy, simple as, bin it.

MOST REBATES ARE FULLY JUSTIFIED:

In reality the vast majority of HB payments that have to be reimbursed to the HB office are payments that have been made by them for a period clearly after the tenant left the property. In other words they didn't put a stop on the rental payments quickly enough.

But you should have been aware the tenant had left, and in that case you should have held on to that money and not paid the landlord for any portion of rental for any period AFTER the tenancy had expired. The rule is:

BENEFIT PAYMENTS RECEIVED FOR A PERIOD AFTER THE TENANCY ENDED ARE INCORRECT. THEY SHOULD NOT BE PASSED TO THE LANDLORD BUT SHOULD BE HELD PENDING REFUND TO THE HB.

In effect, that rental should still be sitting in your client's bank account, (gaining interest for you by the way, so all is not terrible) and you should be able to reimburse the benefit office quickly and fully. Get into the habit of returning overpaid rental to the benefit office whenever they ask for it. If you don't, it could mount up quickly, and they are inclined to become a lot more excited about it, as the numbers increase. It's not unknown for them to appoint outside debt collectors either to chase overpaid cash on their behalf, and that is the last thing you would want.

WHY BOTHER?

After all that, it wouldn't surprise me if you never wanted to hear the words Housing Benefit ever again, yet despite everything, there are still very good reasons not to automatically jettison the idea.

MOST REFERENCED HOUSING BENEFIT TENANTS ARE GREAT – REALLY THEY ARE!

The vast majority of tenants claiming HB are great. I had one with a missing foot, a pretty genuine case there you would think, another who was so badly asthmatic, he couldn't climb the few stairs into our office, I had to meet and greet him in the street when he paid his shortfall which he never once missed, and yet another who'd broken his back when he fell off a crane.

To put it in perspective, out of every fifty HB tenants I dealt with, I would estimate we only ever had a problem with perhaps two or three, and that's not so different to employed tenants.

Anyone, and I mean anyone, can lose their job and they would then normally be entitled to help from the government towards their housing costs. You have to be selective. Some people you take, and some you don't. It's important you don't let your selection standards slip, and keep your wits about you. NEVER take someone on HB that you believe is not being truthful with you, because they are probably not being truthful with the HB office either

And NEVER, EVER house a tenant, or turn a blind eye, knowing full well that an application was in any way fraudulent. You might benefit in the short term. You could end up in clink in the longer term. It is not worth it!

Reference all potential HB tenants in the same manner.
Thoroughly carefully and accurately
Monitor HB payments rigorously
Always collect shortfalls

PRE TENANCY DETERMINATIONS

A pre tenancy determination, a PTD, is a procedure that many tenants in receipt of HB like to follow. In short, it involves the potential tenant filling out a simple one or two page form that is then signed by the landlord or the landlord's agent. You can sign a PTD in the sure and certain knowledge that you are NOT committing yourself, or your landlord, to a tenancy agreement. The potential tenant then lodges the signed PTD form at the benefit office.

The benefit office will examine the form and produce an estimate of the housing benefit they will pay against a particular property. The sole point of a PTD is to assist tenants to check whether they will be able to afford a particular house. The benefit office then send a copy of their estimate to both the tenant and the agent or landlord and they usually turn PTD's around very quickly, within a day or two.

The PTD estimate is not binding, only the final application for Housing Benefit will ascertain that, but it is a useful exercise. For example if a particular house you manage is priced at the equivalent of £100 per a week, and the PTD comes back at £90, you and the tenant would have a good idea that the tenant would need to produce only £10 a week in top-up rent to meet the rental requirement in full. You can discuss with the tenant whether they are comfortable with that, and whether they wish to proceed.

But if the PTD came back at only £40 per week, clearly the tenant would have a much greater shortfall to find, and this might make it difficult for the tenant to proceed. The greater the shortfall, the greater the care you should take before proceeding yourself. You must be confident the tenant has the means to make up any such shortfall. Ask them where it would be coming from?

You should be aware that some landlords are not happy with a PTD being carried out, although they are few and far between. The reason for this is that there have been cases where a landlord may have had a house on at say £100 per week, and a PTD was done and came back, after looking at that particular applicant's individual circumstances at a low figure, of say £35 per week.

There is some evidence to suggest that should that tenant decide not to proceed, and subsequently you located a second tenant and he then requested a PTD, the HB may simply look at their file and say "that house has already been assessed and the figure is £35", in other words at a much lower figure than it would have been if the PTD had not been carried out in the first place.

In my experience, very few landlords object to PTD's, and for the most part they serve a useful purpose both for the tenant and the agent. If in doubt, clear it with the landlord first.

YOU NEED TO DO YOUR HOMEWORK:

I hope I haven't put you off benefit cases altogether because that is not my intention. What I have tried to do is make you more aware of some of the hazards and difficulties that you could come across in your future dealings.

If you decide to consider benefit cases, make the effort to go and visit the benefit office, collect all the bumph they have to offer (and believe me, they have bumph in spades!) Try and make a personal contact there, someone you can talk to for advice and assistance, and then set up a Payment Schedule. This is the vehicle that will transfer funds into your client's account.

The HB will require from you proof of identification among other things, as well as assurance that you are NOT related to the tenants. If the tenant was your niece or aunty, the chances are that you would be barred from collecting the HB. This is because they are very concerned about fraud, and rightly so, and may conclude that you have a conflict of interest, representing a landlord on the one hand, and a tenant, a member of your family on another.

Once you have set up a Schedule, payments will automatically appear in your bank account and will be supported by a hard copy arriving in the post, (once a tenant has successfully completed the necessary paperwork).

Read all the information you can find, and become an expert in completing benefit application forms. Then you can advise others. If the rules say two forms of ID are necessary, there is no point in going to the office with only one, or worse still, none. Everything will come to a standstill. How does that ad go, "it does what it says on the tin!" Housing Benefit forms are the same, if they say they need to see the tenancy agreement; they need to see the tenancy agreement! Don't let the tenant turn up without it. It will only delay things, and you, or they, will have to return again on another day.

Learn, teach yourself, and study, and you will quickly become the biggest expert on HB in your area. You will quickly get to grips with it, and before long you will notice landlords asking you for advice on how the system works, and what they should do next.

Charge them £50 an hour for your advice, I'm serious, you could save a landlord hundreds of pounds with one simple piece of expertise, once you have become that expert. Place it as an additional service in your Fact Pack. "Housing Benefit Consultations: £50".

And one final word: I must emphasise that everything in this chapter is subject to change. HB offices throughout the country may differ, procedures differ too, you know what local bureaucracy is like, they can't leave anything alone for too long. It is for you to keep abreast of changes in your area, no one else can do that for you. So please don't write to me and say, "you said such and such and it's baloney!" I'm telling you exactly as I've found it, but that does not mean you will find it the same where you live.

ARE YOU UP TO THE CHALLENGE?

Aim to become <u>the</u> expert
in all matters housing benefit.
There's a shortage of them, I promise you
Who knows?
you might even derive
some strange satisfaction in doing so.

Chapter 15 : Your Business Progresses

You've launched your business, your advertising campaign is well under way, and you have let your first property, trousering your first fees. You've learnt a great deal about your local housing benefit systems, and that might be something you never expected to know. But how is your business progressing, and what can you do to push it along?

There will be days when nothing seems to happen, the phone doesn't ring, a landlord you may have had great hopes for has chosen another. They can be fussy devils, and you have to expect that sometimes. You might start to become a little disillusioned, depressed even, and when that happens you must recognise the signs and SNAP OUT OF IT! STOP FEELING SORRY FOR YOURSELF. MAKE THINGS HAPPEN! It is your business, and you must drive it. No one else will.

You can take comfort from the fact that every businessperson feels like that sometimes. There are some days when it's more difficult to motivate oneself than others. Your mind starts to drift away to how nice it would be to lie on the beach in Barcelona. (Is there a beach in Barcelona? I don't know).

But it's precisely on days like these when nothing much seems to happen, that you should be aggressively promoting your business, for the simple reason that you have the time to do so.

PROMOTE YOUR BUSINESS FEROCIOUSLY:

Take a look at every tenant's application form you have ever received, whether you have rejected the tenant or not, you will find one and possibly two landlord's names and addresses on each one. Dig the forms out and take another butchers. Landlord's right? Remember when you first started and you were wondering how you could contact real landlords, people with property; and there they are, staring you in the face. Turn on your word processor and write them a letter, do it today.

Dear Landlord, except you might write:

Dear Mister Ramsbottom,

I am writing you a brief note today to advise you we have several excellent fully employed tenants on our books seeking property in this area right now.

(If you have been advertising in the papers during the previous four weeks you will most certainly have a supply of excellent potential tenants. Did you note their names and telephone numbers down? You should have done.)

Do you have any property currently available to let? If so, we would like to offer you a 20% *(the incentive figure can be anything you like, it's your business you are in total control)* deduction on our normal fees. Please ring me at any time on my private number 07000 00000 to discuss the matter. I look forward to hearing from you.

Yours sincerely
Jack Boeing
Jets Lets.

Get the letters in the post quickly, not in a few days time but today! If you post ten letters to ten landlords, I'll bet you get a call back, at least one. Remember, every signed up landlord should produce at least a £1,000 per year in revenue for you.

It will be worth your while to pursue them. It's a good idea to include an insurance brochure too. Even if the landlord has no property to let, he might need some additional insurance, and if he rings you and not Farquar's Lettings up the road, it's a positive sign he's thinking about you. Your aim is to encourage your local landlords to ring you about all their property matters, and if you contact them on a regular basis, sooner or later, they will.

When times are quiet it is up to you to MAKE THINGS HAPPEN, no one else will. It's your business, and it is YOU who must kick up the dust. Be imaginative; study other agent's promotional schemes. Come up with something different, something BETTER, but whatever you do, keep yourself busy promoting your agency, because your agency will become the best agency in the town. You know that, I know that, it's your task to demonstrate the fact to others.

YOU WILL BECOME
THE BEST AGENCY IN THE TOWN
NOTHING WILL STOP YOU!
BELIEVE IT
AND IT WILL HAPPEN

TRY SIGNS:

Another excellent way of promoting and advertising your business is to have some signs professionally made up. You know the things I mean, like the estate agents stick up outside houses all over your area. But I wouldn't recommend having them erected outside the property for two reasons. Firstly it's usual to pay an outside contractor to erect these signs and right from the beginning we have concentrated on ways to cut out unnecessary overheads. It's not cheap and it's a cost you can do without.

Secondly, signs left outside can and do go missing, especially around November 5th. Instead, keep a supply in the boot of your car, and whenever you're instructed to let a property, place a sign in the front window of the house, facing the road. Make sure the telephone number can be clearly seen from the street. For good orders sake it's a good idea to confirm with the owner if it's all right to do so. Once you have paid the initial costs of the signs this is a fantastic way to promote your business and it costs you absolutely nothing.

It will give you a real buzz to suddenly see your signs appearing in windows all over the town. I have let hundreds of properties using signs like these, and you can too. They can be just as effective as newspaper advertising and are much more cost efficient. Keeping them indoors means they are not going to get vandalised or go missing, and they can be used again and again and again. Just remember once you've let the property, to pick them up and take them with you for next time.

Take care where you buy them too, I have seen some ridiculous prices being quoted for the normal sized estate agency signs, and it is the usual size you want. Over £50 each I was quoted by one firm, each! When I last bought signs I bought a hundred for £250, admittedly it was a little while ago, but they were the best buy I ever made. They work; they let houses, and are so much cheaper than newspaper advertising. In addition the more signs you put up, the more chance you have of landlords noticing them too and thinking, "my, this is an expanding go-ahead company, perhaps I should give them a try!"

You'll find a brief list of letting and estate agent's sign makers at the end of this publication, or alternatively run a quick internet search on google.

YOUR OWN PROPERTY PORTFOLIO:

And what about your own property register? Never forget the importance of creating your own portfolio. If you haven't started yet, due to lack of finance, the objective must be to put money aside regularly to accumulate that first deposit.

I can't tell you how excited I was when I started refurbishing my first buy-to-let. I think it must have been just before those property makeover shows started that now cram the TV schedules. Have you noticed they all say the same things? Keep the walls and carpets neutral, creams and whites, beige and light. Crikey it's so neutral I'm practically falling asleep.

Well I didn't do my house in creams and white and beige and light. I worked like a Trojan, every weekend and most evenings too. It was an old house, but big with high ceilings and that means hard work I can tell you. When I'd finished papering and painting I bought the carpets. A lush rich maroon for the hall, landing and stairs contrasting with the Victorian style green patterned wallpaper. In the front room I laid a royal blue carpet to contrast with the yellow walls. I stood back, hands on hips and admired my handiwork. I thought it looked the bees.

The house appeared in my ad the following week and six people immediately showed interest. I couldn't wait to show the first potential tenant round. A neat attractive young woman arrived carrying a bonny baby girl and bounced into the hall smiling. She looked down the hall and up the stairs, without comment, and hurried into the living room. She looked around again and laughed noisily through her sealed lips.

"What do you think?" I asked excitedly.

"The house is great, but not the colours!" She laughed again. "Who chose them? He must have been a loony!"

I didn't dare mention that I'd chosen the colours, I didn't see the point. She said she couldn't possibly live there, as she'd have to redo everything. But I let the house soon after that, and it has been full ever since. I never go there now. I've heard from the gas safety man that the tenant has redecorated the house from top to bottom, in off white, and beige, really nice it is, so the gasman says. Perhaps the less extreme makeover shows do have a point after all. Keep it neutral.

Then my dad died and left me his house. I was going to sell it, but almost at the last minute had second thoughts. Instead I set about refurbishing that one too, ready for the rental market. No bright colours this time, creams and beige in abundance.

It took me a month and I did everything myself and by the time I'd finished I was spent, I can tell you, in more ways than one, not to mention a ricked shoulder that took months to heal. My first viewer appeared the very next day, an older refined lady. I showed her round and she never said a word, never a hint of how she felt about it. I showed her into the bathroom and she took a step backwards and looked at me disdainfully.

"What?" I said.

" I hope you're going to do something about that!"

"What?" I repeated.

"The bath of course, you ARE going to be replacing that aren't you? Surely you don't expect me to get into that! No-one in their right mind would get into a bath like that!"

The bath was a large roll-top standalone tub, the kind that have come right back into fashion in recent times, you see them in every DIY superstore nowadays. At one end of the bath were two huge old silver taps that looked like Queen Victoria might have used. I thought they had character.

I looked back at the bath and then at her and I didn't have the courage to tell her I had wallowed happily in that very bath for a full hour after I'd finished painting the kitchen barely two days before. She stormed out and left me standing there. I didn't change the bath, and the house let shortly afterwards. Houses do let. As my good friend Michael is fond of saying, "there is a bum for every seat".

PROPERTIES DO LET:

Providing a property is in reasonable condition in a safe area, it will let. Trust me. Remember, everyone has different tastes with regard to colours and decorating, it would be a dull world if we all liked the same thing.

Start thinking about your own properties that you are going to let when you can afford it. Visit the DIY warehouses. Check out the bathrooms and the kitchens. Become an expert. Make plans, and remember that kitchens and bathrooms do not have to cost an absolute fortune. Don't ever buy the cheapest, but buying the very dearest is a mistake too, unless you are aiming at the very top liner rentals. If you are not going to recoup the money you spend on the property through improved rental figures, why spend it?

Think about accruing deposits
Think about acquiring houses
THINK BIG
THINK

Chapter 16: Computer Programs & the Internet

Fifteen years ago almost no one had the Internet in their home. Now practically everyone I know does. Twenty years ago almost no one had a PC at home, I know that for a fact because I started selling them.

"A PC, what's a PC? Haven't you got any Amiga's or Atari's?"
That was a typical riposte to my urging my customers to buy PC's.
"PC's are the coming thing", I said, but not many people believed me.

Now almost everyone has a PC at home. So what are they using all this sophisticated and powerful equipment for?

To look for property of course! Property websites are now the second most frequently accessed sites on the entire web. (I'll give you one guess what the foremost is, but we won't go there!) Think property please. Every estate agent has a web site; many agents have more than one. Most letting agents have a web site and if you aspire to becoming a successful letting agent you must seriously consider a web site too.

Why? Because they offer unlimited worldwide advertising with as many colour pictures as you like that can be accessed anywhere on earth for very low cost, comparatively speaking. Compare for a moment the cost of a small display ad in the local paper. Perhaps £130 and in a few days it's gone forever. Your web site is on, all the time, 24 hours a day, 365 days a year. You MUST have access to the web, clued up landlords expect it, and tenants now use it locate rental property.

It only remains for you to decide which type of site to go for. Broadly speaking you have four choices:

1. Your own bespoke site. Individually designed to your requirements incorporating precisely the features you want

2. An off the shelf site you could adapt to your own use

3. Rent space on other larger property sites

4. Create your own site

YOUR OWN BESPOKE SITE:

If you have the money, you might like to look at the first option. But it will cost you a fair amount of cash, I saw one firm quoting £1,000 in today's daily paper, and one small word of warning. Make certain when the site name is registered YOU OWN the site outright. A friend of mine had an antiques site and after a while he became dissatisfied with his site hosting company. So he gave notice to terminate the contract and move to another host.

A few days later he received an email from his service provider politely telling him that he could certainly move, but the site name would be staying with the host because they had registered and still owned the web site name. Despite the fact my friend had spent thousands of pounds promoting the name, and owned the actual physical business shipping antiques worldwide, he discovered he didn't own his own web site.

Cheekily the host offered to sell it to him, for a thousand pounds. He declined. When you start your own web site, make absolutely certain it is YOU who owns the name. There is nothing worse than spending time and money building up a successful site, only to discover that you don't in fact have any ongoing rights to it.

Before you buy shop around and then haggle, for there is a huge range of companies offering sites at greatly differing prices. Check out some of the sites they have previously prepared and ask yourself are they really good enough? There has been a huge leap forward in the quality of sites in the past year or two and there is no excuse now for any site to look cheap, nasty, and homemade, especially if it isn't.

ADAPTING AN EXISTING PACKAGE:

Option 2 is something I used for a while. If you look in Exchange and Mart there is a company advertising Internet business opportunities in there called www. fast-data.co.uk. Among their off the shelf web sites is a property site. I used one for nearly two years and adapted it quite successfully to my own use. The site was reasonably priced, easily adaptable and it was efficiently run, in that it was very rarely down (unavailable, or off line).

You might like to have a look at it, because it could suit your requirements. The site also provided a service you could offer to the general public whereby they could advertise their own properties to let or for sale on your site. Of course they had to pay you for the privilege to do so.

Perhaps you also know a landlord who doesn't want to use an agent for most of their business but would not be averse to advertising their properties on the internet. You can fix your site advertising fees as high or as low as you wish, but it's a good idea to set them competitively to begin with, to attract a quantity of properties onto the site.

Don't forget, the more properties and information on the site, the more interesting it will be to viewers. The longer a browser is gazing at your web pages, the more likely they are to purchase one of your services. The trick to keeping them connected is to make sure there is loads of content, and interesting content at that.

Be bold, and write to five or six other smaller independent agencies both in your area and further afield. (There will soon be lots of smaller agents than you.) Some of these agents will not have a web site of their own and you will be able to offer them the facility of putting ALL their properties (an unlimited number) on your site including a colour photograph for a small fixed fee.

Perhaps you could charge them £75 per month, payable by standing order into your account, to allow them to put their properties on your site, regardless of quantity. They would actually do all the uploading too, it's simple to do, and you would not have to do a thing, other than check their money was in your bank account every month. If you signed up ten agents at £75 per month, that would produce over a year, a more than useful £9,000, yet another possible way for you to raise your property deposits.

If you were going to offer this service to other agents it would be a good idea not to call your web site by the name you were trading as. For example if you were trading as BRENT'S RENTS other agents would be unlikely to feel comfortable placing their houses on a site of the same name.

However if you chose a more general title, such as SMARTPROPERTY or PROPERTYEXPRESS or SOUTHCOASTHOMES or HUNTAHOME (subject to the names being available), other independent agencies would be more likely to use your site. Again you could charge whatever you liked. Your initial aim would be to get as much interesting content on to the site, and as quickly as possible, which in turn would attract the required traffic, which in turn again, would attract more users. It's that snowball effect again.

RENT SPACE ON OTHER PROPERTY SITES:

The third alternative web presence is to rent space on an existing site and I suspect initially this may be the best option for you. There are a countless number of sites now available ranging from the very famous rightmove.co.uk and assertahomes.co.uk down to specialist rental only sites. No doubt the bigger sites will be quite expensive if you can get on them, but they do have thousands and thousands of hits every day. That's what you want of course, lots of hits, readers, call it what you will.

You might also like to check out Fish4homes, Ukhomes4sale, and Property Renting Online; their web addresses are all listed in the directory of contacts at the end of this book. The Internet, despite its problems and patience testing qualities is here to stay. Get involved, get organised, get noticed, and most importantly get your properties on line.

CREATE YOUR OWN WEBSITE:

If you have any web-designing expertise this will undoubtedly be an area that you have already considered. If you have little or no website designer know-how you have probably discounted this idea. But hang on a moment. If you have a computer and a little experience you can design your own website quite easily and there are very good reasons to do so.

You could sign up to one of the many new off the shelf services that provide you with an excellent variety of templates to choose from. You can then design your site to fit in with your own operation, in your own house colours, and it is not expensive.

In fact prices have dropped heavily in the past two years and you could put together a professional site for less than a hundred pounds. It seems incredible, but it's true, especially when you think back to the cost of a decent site five or ten years ago. Check out this site for starters. www.partnershop.co.uk/shop/1598.

On there you will find that new web names can be registered for as little as £2! A few years ago you would have paid £50 or more. You can also have your site hosted for as little as £4 per month. Incredible isn't it. And they will supply you with everything you need to get started.

The service is run by Lycos, the giant Internet company, you have probably heard of them, they advertise on the TV regularly and use the black Labrador as their logo. It's good to be involved with larger well establish companies, especially in the field of internet, where seemingly hundreds of businesses come and go every year.

ADDITIONAL REVENUE STREAMS:

We have already touched on two potential new income streams, selling property advertising space on your sites, and offering the use of your site to other agents, but it doesn't stop there. You can also earn very useful commission and give your site extra kudos by running banner ads from other companies. If you joined one of the affiliate marketing companies that abound on the web, you will have no shortage of high profile ads that you can run.

Top line firms too like COMET, BRITISH GAS, and BOOTS.

But even better than that, if you incorporated the banner ads of Holiday Cottage Companies, like Stilwells and English Country Cottages, you would give your site readers the ability to click through to browse thousands of cottages not just in Britain but in France, Ireland, and Spain too. Why would you want to do this? Money of course!

Once you sign up with an affiliate marketing company and load up banners, (the computer software firm will supply you with everything you need to be able to do this), every time a reader clicks through from your site and books a holiday cottage, you receive a commission. Typically this can range from £5 to £10 per booking, which isn't huge, but remember, once you have set up the banner ads you don't have to do anything else, but count the cash. It simply drops into your bank account once a month. It's another income stream you have up and running and earning money for you. Once you set it up, you can forget all about it.

When you are publicising your site and your business you could also announce "thousands of holiday cottages available now". Even if you haven't yet hundreds of empty and available properties of your own, your readers will still have the opportunity of clicking through and checking out hundreds and hundreds of interesting properties.

It's a great service to offer your clients. It makes your site and your business much more interesting and has cost you almost nothing to set up. No agency fees, nothing. It will keep your clients on your site, it will keep them coming back, and it will get people talking about you.

You'll find details of affiliate marketing companies in the trade directory at the back of this book, but you will receive full details of these services from the software company if you decide to sign up with them.

UPDATE YOUR WEB SITE:

Make sure you update your site regularly, daily if you possibly can. There is nothing worse than viewing a site and it says something like, "Site last updated August 16th", when it's February. I actually saw a site the other day that proudly said: "last updated July 15th 1999. As I write, it's summer 2005!

And when your site is finished and ready, remember the most important thing to do, is to promote it. There is no point in having a brilliant site that no one knows about. Put your web address on absolutely everything, your letterheads, your business cards and compliment slips, your shop window ads, your fact pack, your signs, on the back of your car, even at the foot of your emails. (But don't spam! Spam is sending out uninvited cold calling emails. That is now illegal in Great Britain.)

But you could put an additional message at the foot of all your usual outgoing emails, "Properties to let now on www.prowseshouses.co.uk" or something similar. But the most important place to publicise your web site address is within your weekly newspaper advertising in as large size letters as space permits.

It is from here that you will generate the vast majority of your hits. People use the web more and more with each passing month, especially for anything to do with property matters. I read the other day that 78,000 new users are joining the web worldwide EVERY DAY. People will look at your site. When they do, hook 'em!

PROPERTY MANAGEMENT SOFTWARE:

Selecting which computer software you are going to use is an important decision and shouldn't be rushed. Check out everything that is available because it is very difficult, time consuming, and expensive, to switch horses at a later date.

For small and medium sized business accounts, Sage is now the undisputed market leader. All accountants know how it works inside out and it will speed up your annual audit, but before you dash out and buy Sage, consider purchasing or leasing a full property package, because many of these include accounting software. Quickbooks too is another package that many small businesses use.

Probably the most famous and widely used lettings package today is called CARL. Computer Aided Residential Lettings, though there are many other packages available. CARL is based in Shaw, near Oldham up on the edge of the Pennines. They now have hundreds of users throughout the UK and because they have such a broad user base, they have been able to introduce many sophisticated improvements into the system in recent years.

I believe they are still operating on the basis that you cannot buy the system outright but rent or lease it on a monthly basis. You will find their web site listed in the trade directory at the end of this book. They offer training, both on site and in house, and any number of seminars that are very useful. They offer software that produces contracts, dozens of different standard letters, sections on housing benefit, fact packs, and so much more paperwork, some of which you undoubtedly will never use.

I don't know whether they offer web site services as well but it would not surprise me if they did. Whether you go with them or not, please do take a look at the product, and

155

their web site, it will broaden your mind immensely as to what is available. Ask for a FREE sample disk and you will see for yourself what it can do. It's not perfect, computer programs rarely are, but it has a tremendous amount to offer.

Other property software products you might consider are Rentacomm, Key data, and Professional Property Letting. I know absolutely nothing of these products; you will find their web names in the trade directory at the end of this book. Check them out thoroughly, and if you are considering signing up with them, ask them to supply you with the addresses of some satisfied customers. As they say on the stock market bulletin boards, DYOR, do your own research. If they can't or won't supply you with satisfied customers to check out, use someone else.

Get Connected
A Web Presence is Essential
Check out Property Software
DYOR

Chapter 17: Gas & Electrical Safety Checks

As an agent or property owner, you have a direct responsibility to ensure that there is a Gas Safety Certificate on your file BEFORE you place a tenant into a property.

NEVER put a tenant into a property where there is gas, unless you have a gas safety certificate on your file, or have had sight of a valid certificate. In that case obtain a photocopy for your file.

THE HISTORY OF CORGI:

Gas Safety Inspections MUST be carried out ANNUALLY and MUST be carried out by a suitably qualified CORGI registered engineer. Corgi stands for the Confederation for the Registration of Gas Installers. It came into being in 1970 following the disaster at Ronan Point, the 22 storey block of flats in east London that was devastated by a massive gas blast in 1968.

That disaster claimed five lives and led to a determination to protect the general public from unsafe gas appliances. Today there are approximately 44,000 registered companies belonging to CORGI employing just under 100,000 operatives. Only a CORGI registered plumber may issue a gas safety certificate. Check on the certificate for the CORGI logo. One copy of the certificate should be left in the property with the tenant, and another retained on file in the Agent's office.

If a landlord refuses to produce a certificate you must either arrange for one to be completed yourself, and deduct the cost of it from the landlord's account, stating that it is a legal requirement to do so, or alternatively, <u>DON'T LET THE PROPERTY.</u>

There is no room for manoeuvre on this issue. If you failed to produce a certificate should there be a spot check, which there sometimes are, or God forbid there was a serious incident in one of the properties that you managed, you and the landlord would be in serious trouble.

<u>SEVERE PENALTIES FOR NON-COMPLIANCE:</u>

It is not unknown for a prison sentence to be imposed on parties who do not adhere to this vitally important procedure. Unbelievably some greedy landlords still try and get away with not incurring this expense. If you let the property, you MUST make sure a Gas Safety Certificate is in place. Remember to mark the tenancy start date on your file too, and diarise it, so that a new certificate is arranged next year when it is due. Like car tax disks, they are only valid for one year.

If you don't adhere to this legislation how would you like to explain to distressed parents that their young son or daughter was gassed to death in one of the properties you managed because you couldn't be bothered to spend £50 or so to have the gas appliances checked? Exactly, you wouldn't. For me, this is the single most important point on any property you intend to let.

Find a Corgi Registered Plumber. Get a Certificate BEFORE you move anyone into the house. It's simple; make sure it's done. And don't forget to charge the landlord for all costs incurred.

ELECTRICAL SAFETY:

Electrical safety in any property is not quite so clear-cut, in that you are not responsible for having an annual check and certificate on file. However both the agent, and the landlord have a duty of care towards the tenant to ensure the electrics are checked and safe.

On all let property you must ensure that the electrical system and all appliances supplied are safe - failure to comply with the regulations is a criminal offence and could result in:

- A fine of £5,000 per item for not complying

- Six month's imprisonment

- Possible manslaughter charges in the event of deaths

- The tenant may also sue the agent and the landlord for civil damages

- Your property insurance could also be invalidated. The Health & Safety Executive enforces the regulations. There is no statutory requirement to have annual safety checks on electrical equipment as there is with gas, but it is advisable for landlords to have periodic checks carried out by a qualified electrician.

I suggest you discuss the matter with your landlord and if there is any doubt, especially if you notice worn cabling, loose plugs and sockets, and dated equipment you should insist those matters are addressed immediately. Don't take any risks; in the longer run your landlords will thank you for keeping them straight and legal. THINK SAFETY – ALWAYS. This is NOT an area where monetary savings can ever be made.

Would you put up with dodgy electrics in your own home? Of course you wouldn't! Neither should anyone else.

FURNITURE FIRE SAFETY:

There is one other aspect of SAFETY you need to bear in mind and that is FIRE SAFETY particularly to do with fire retardant furniture.

Where a property is furnished the landlord may only supply soft furnishings where they comply with the latest fire safety regulations. This particularly relates to foam filled furniture that must bear the fire retardant kite mark. If it does not, this furniture must not be supplied to the tenant.

You as the agent have a responsibility to check that there is no illegal furniture within the premises and if you find any that is, it is your duty to advise the landlord to have it removed. This especially applies to settees, sofas, chairs and beds.

Most landlords are fully aware of their responsibilities when it comes to providing modern fire resistant furniture. The easiest thing to do to comply with this legislation is to have any old foam filled furniture removed and taken to the local tip. Charity shops will not touch it for precisely the same reason. This is one of the main reasons why so many landlords prefer to supply unfurnished property. If there's no furniture in the house, you can't break any fire safety rules.

Double-check it. Does the property include any soft furniture that does not bear the kitemarks? If it does, advise the landlord to remove or replace it. If they won't, and the let goes ahead both YOU and the LANDLORD could be held accountable if there was a fire during the time of the tenancy. Why take the risk? Never put old foam filled furniture into any property you may own. You would be far better off to let the property unfurnished, even if the rental figure was slightly less. You are talking life and death here, it is as important as that. Penalties are rightly harsh for transgressors. Make sure you understand your responsibilities. Keep legal, keep safe.

Finally, there is a new requirement that instruction manuals and booklets are left in the property for all gas and electrical appliances. It's a good idea to establish a file containing these booklets in the kitchen drawer. You can point them out to tenants when they move in. Make sure they are still there when the tenant moves out again.

SAFETY IS PARAMOUNT
IT GOES WITHOUT SAYING

Chapter 18: Additional Revenue Streams

To date we have discussed nine potential income streams, namely:

1. Tenant's processing Fees
2. Landlord's one off fee on managed properties
3. Landlord's monthly management percentage fee
4. Landlord's one off fee on unmanaged properties
5. Inventory Fees
6. Housing Benefit Consultation Fees
7. Interest on deposits
8. Selling advertising on your web site
9. Commission gained through click throughs on your web site

But it doesn't end there. Here are another four potential income streams that you can establish and build up very quickly for little outlay. Don't worry if some credits are only small to begin with, it's all grist to the mill, and as your business grows, so will many of these streams. Confucius he say, "Many streams make a flood". Well I don't suppose he did, but he might have.

INSURANCE

You really should be selling insurance policies from day one. Why? Because they entail very little work, and policies can run on for years and years. Many landlords opt to pay their property insurance premiums by monthly direct debit and every time they do, you get a payment.

Every year they renew, you get a payment. Typical commission is 20% of the total premiums. That may not sound a lot by itself, but look at this:

With the huge increase in house prices over the past three or four years, and the increase anyway in insurance premiums, a typical let semi detached house now costs around £500 per year to insure. If you have a hundred properties on your book, and if you work at it, you will reach that figure sooner than you think, and if you insured them all, that's 20% of £50,000, that's £10,000 a year, EVERY YEAR! That ten grand would be paid straight into your bank account. That ten grand could be the deposit on your very first property to let, and the beauty is, you wouldn't have done that much to earn it. Sell insurance, it makes sense.

The commission is transferred directly into your bank account, or you deduct it at source. You get paid for filling out one form. In the second year you get paid for doing absolutely nothing. Every year that policy is renewed, you get paid, and some policies will run on for ten or fifteen years.

Besides landlord's buildings insurance, there are numerous other policies available, such as tenant's contents, landlord's legal expenses and many others. I made a point of writing to every new tenant after they'd moved in welcoming them to the property, an up beat happy kind of letter, and I enclosed a tenant's contents insurance policy brochure.

One agent I know actually sends his tenants one of those greetings card type things, "Hope you are Happy in you New Home". He tucks an insurance brochure inside. The tenant might send off the application form direct to the insurer together with their cheque and you probably won't even know about it, until a payment shows up in your bank account from your grateful insurance broker. Do it, it works, it really does.

Incidentally, with regard to contents, especially in furnished or part furnished properties, the landlord is responsible for insuring <u>their</u> contents; the tenant is responsible for insuring <u>theirs</u>. So if you see a tenant moving in a giant sized expensive television, do them a favour and advise them to make sure they get insured. "Oh and by the way, here's a brochure, why don't you fill it in and send it off, pay it monthly if you prefer, it's only a few pounds". They do it, and you get paid. You'll also be in line for a big thank you, if they ever get burgled.

Keep a small supply of insurance brochures in the car: you never know when you might need one. They are FREE when you sign up with one of the big agencies.

BUY-TO-LET MORTGAGES

Oh no! I hear you cry, I don't want to get involved in mortgages. The good news is you don't have to. All you need do is hand out buy-to-let mortgage brochures to new and existing landlords, and to anyone you think might be interested in buying property for letting or living purposes.

Everything is then arranged directly between the mortgage provider and the person taking out the mortgage. Your only involvement is to distribute brochures bearing your identity and admire the commission that dumps into your bank account. This commission can easily top a thousand pounds on a single mortgage! Worth handing out a brochure for don't you think? Where can you obtain the brochures? Try Homelet.

UTILITY SUPPLIES

Telephones, gas, electricity and Internet. You can reduce your landlords and your own costs on all of these. How? By introducing them to Telecom Plus. Telecom Plus is a hugely successful PLC based in London. They have been established for six years and are quoted on the London Stock Exchange. They provide reduced priced utilities including, to their telephony customers, the lowest priced gas and electricity in the UK, GUARANTEED. In effect they are supplying end users with power and phones at wholesale prices.

The clients do not need to change their supply equipment. There is no interruption to service, no contract to sign, meaning that the user can return to their traditional supplier at any time, and no numbers or codes to dial on land line telephone calls.

You can easily incorporate an agency into your business and earn commissions on all the customers you introduce. You are in an excellent position to do so. You can save your clients money on all their gas, electricity and telephones in all of their properties. You could send a brochure to your tenants too, along with the one for insurance. Everyone wants extra money in their pockets don't they? Signing up with Telecom Plus will give you and your clients precisely that.

And when you start to build your own portfolio, make sure your own houses are all switched to Telecom Plus too. You'll reduce your costs, and pick up a commission. You can check out how to become an agent and look at loads of information on www.telecomplus.org.uk/676159.

Don't forget to switch over your office utilities too, the more customers and users you have, including your own, the more commission you will make, and the more money you will save.

PROPERTY REPAIRS

Every property you own or manage will require repairs sooner or later, and you need to establish your own system to deal with them. Imagine an irritated tenant who rings you first thing in the morning and complains that they have been without electricity since 8pm the previous night. What do you do?

Check the file to ascertain if there are instructions there as to who will sort maintenance problems. If you manage the property for a landlord you should have discussed with them at the outset who would deal with maintenance. If you are instructed to sort the problem, consider whether there is a trip switch in the property. It could be something very simple, such as a blown light bulb that may have set the trip switch, turning off all the electricity.

You'll usually find the switch in the main electricity cupboard. It happens quite often in my house, usually on a cold dark January night when a bulb pops. My electrical cupboard happens to be outside on the side of the house, not just the meter but the fuses as well. My electrician tells me that modern systems are deliberately designed that way as a safety feature, to trip the electric, hair trigger, they're meant to do it.

If there is a trip switch, you may already know where it is. You could ask the tenant to flip it back and the problem is often solved. If there isn't a switch, or turning the switch hasn't solved the problem, you obviously need the services of a qualified electrician.

It's always a good idea to discuss with any landlord prior to letting a property the procedures for dealing with repairs. Many landlords, especially the larger ones have their own maintenance man, or even a team of trade people standing by for just such an emergency. In that case all you need do is ring the landlord and report the problem, and they should deal with it. If the tenant is without electricity you should emphasise the urgency of the matter, if you don't, the repair guy might take his time arriving, and in that case, you will certainly be on the end of increasingly heated telephone calls.

Where the landlord does not have any arrangement in place to deal with maintenance matters, they might ask you to deal with it. That is a very good reason to build up your own network of contacts of electricians, plumbers, decorators, joiners, and sundry workmen. Keep their numbers handy, and when you find one who is prompt, reliable and inexpensive, look after them, for they are like gold dust.

When their bill comes in, deduct it from the landlord's statement and pay the contractor as soon as you are able to do so. Build up goodwill, for there will come a time when you need help to sort out a problem at short notice. Contractors who haven't been promptly paid are unlikely to be sympathetic.

YOUR OWN MAINTENANCE DIVISION:

You will find the quantity of maintenance jobs you deal with steadily increases and sooner or later the thought will occur to you that you should be carrying out the work yourself, instead of farming it out. You'd have more control over the situation if you delegated one of your own staff to sort matters. BRENTS RENTS for example might set up another division, say BRENTS PROPERTY

167

MAINTENANCE, to deal with the work that pours in. As you become more confident in overseeing maintenance contracts, you could take on additional work from outside customers too. Do you smell revenue? You should.

Of course you will need suitably qualified staff to carry out the work, perhaps a brother or relative, and you might even employ some of the same guys you used on a sub contracting basis before. If you do that, you should negotiate a trade discount, so you can pass on more or less the same charges to the landlord as before.

TAKING A MARGIN:

I don't have a problem with an agent taking a margin on maintenance work, providing it is reasonable. If you are spending a great deal of time organising and solving landlord's repair problems you are, in my view, entitled to be paid for your time and expertise. You are a professional person, and if there is a small percentage mark up to cover your time, that must be fair and reasonable.

However, it has to be said that some agents abuse their position when it comes to repairs, and eventually this abuse has a habit of coming to the landlord's attention, and before you know it you have a very dissatisfied client.

One agent I knew charged his landlord £700 for having the outside of his house painted, that was the window frames, gables and soffits, not the rendering. I know for a fact that he beat a desperate local painter down to just £200 to have the work done. If you are completing work for third parties you are free to quote any price you like, and make as much margin as you can, and good luck to you. But if you are carrying out work for your own landlords, whilst at the same time taking a huge margin for yourself, there could be a conflict of interest.

Remember, you do have a duty of care towards your landlord, he is employing you to look after his property interests, and clearly that does not include ripping him off with huge margins, as in that painting job.

The acid test is to ask yourself whether you would be comfortable for all the facts on any repair to be laid on the table in front of the property owner. If you were not, perhaps you should be questioning how much mark-up you were incorporating for yourself. Was it justified to cover the time element spent? You will know the answer, better than anyone else.

Remember, if you rip off a landlord, and they discover the fact, you might kiss goodbye to his business forever, perhaps rightly too, and quite possibly to all his friends as well.

USEFUL INCOME STREAM:

Nevertheless you could build up a very useful additional revenue stream by establishing a repairs and maintenance wing to your business. One agency I knew made more money from their repairs division than they ever did from property management, which might give you a flavour of what could be achieved.

There are never enough companies to go round in this field, especially in times of emergency. For example after severe gales, when there are numerous repair jobs to be picked up, such as tiles off and fences down.

If you are running a property management agency you will become embroiled in sorting out maintenance matters, whether you like it or not. Treat the opportunity professionally. Get organised, recruit good quality tradesmen, pay them promptly, and make sure your time is adequately rewarded.

You can expand and develop your maintenance division too, perhaps when property management may be going through a quieter spell. You are not, and never have been, a one trick pony, and this is a real opportunity to create additional income for very little outlay.

Establish New Revenue Streams
Consider Insurance Policies &
Mortgage Introductions
Reduce Your Utility Bills
Build Up a Network of Good Maintenance People
Establish Your Own Repairs Division

Chapter 19: Dealing With Difficult Tenants

Far and away the best way to deal with troublesome tenants, is not to have any in the first place. It's a fact that providing you carry out your referencing procedures thoroughly, you will weed out the vast majority of bad tenants. Indeed you might be surprised at how few difficult customers you ever come across.

Nevertheless, sooner or a later, you will land yourself with a problem tenant, the nightmare person you'd always imagined. You can take comfort from the fact that every agent does so sooner or later, even the very largest and strongest, and the very best. There isn't an agent alive who hasn't experienced a bad tenant at some point in their commercial career. If they say they haven't, they're lying. The acid test will be to see how you deal with the problem.

TYPES OF BAD TENANT:

Troublesome tenants come in six fishy flavours.

1. The rowdy snappy piranha, who upsets the neighbours

2. The disappearing dogfish, who does a runner

3. The sprat who can't, or won't, pay the rent

4. The destroyer shark, who damages or wrecks the place

5. The moaning marling, who will find fault with everything

6. The barnacle, who downs anchors and refuses to move

The moment you become aware you have a problem, it is most important you deal with it at the earliest opportunity. If you leave it to fester, more often than not, it will only get worse. So how do you handle problem lets, and problem tenants? Here are a few suggestions.

1. THE NOISY TENANT

If you receive telephoned or written complaints from neighbours about excessive noise, you need to write to the tenant immediately. But before you fire off a missive, bear in mind that you only have the neighbour's word regarding the problem, and sometimes neighbours can be as naughty and mischievous as any tenant.

Some neighbours think that people who rent property are beneath them and shouldn't be allowed to live next door in their swanky neighbourhood. Some neighbours will do anything to have renters moved on. Bear that in mind.

Your letter should reflect this possibility. I suggest wording along the lines of, "we have received a complaint (s) regarding excessive noise and late night disturbances. IF this is indeed the case, please do all you can to ensure there is no repetition".

The words 'IF THIS IS INDEED THE CASE,' are the most important. Some tenants on receiving such a letter will realise they have been a little noisy, and will keep quieter in the future. Often you'll never hear a thing about it again. But it's more likely they will ring the office looking for a row. "How dare you write a letter like this accusing me of all sorts", would be a typical riposte, and occasionally a great deal ruder!

You politely point out that you haven't accused anyone of anything, you clearly said IF there was a disturbance. You should then move the conversation on to ask if they heard anything? Was there a problem in the road? Drunks perhaps?

Should you subsequently receive a second complaint you have no alternative but to write to the tenant again detailing further complaints. You may need to state that should there be further problems you may have to take steps to bring the tenancy to an end.

With a little luck the tenancy may well be nearing an end anyway, and if it is coming up for renewal, you have the handy option not to renew. Think very carefully about renewing tenancies with noisy tenants, and if you have to extend, do so for the shortest possible period. In that case the tenancy is running on, in effect, on a further trial basis. Further problems, and you could bring it to an end. Never grant a long-term renewal to a tenant about whom you have received numerous complaints. Move them on instead, and solve the problem that way.

2: MIDNIGHT FLITTERS

The disappearing tenant is a problem, albeit a rare one, but at least they are out of the house. Solve the problem by re-letting the property as quickly as possible, as long as the landlord has instructed you so to do. If there is a dilapidation bill for damages incurred, you could try to locate the departed tenant, but you might find that harder than you think.

You could employ an outside agency to try and track them down, but that costs money. More often than not you would be throwing good money after bad. Consider cutting your losses, that's the advice we would give the landlord, although the total value of any outstanding claim would need to be considered.

Remember too, to examine any valid insurance policies. They may well cover the landlord against midnight flitters. If the landlord hasn't taken out any insurance, now might be a good time to try and sell them a policy for the future. Remind them of the merits of such a policy. Most landlords will reinvest a little of their rental income in insurance, if you highlight the benefits. So why not through you?

3: NON-PAYERS

The non-payer of rent is always a challenge for any agent. I go back to the referencing stage again. If the references were good, non-payment of rent is a surprisingly rare event. Yes, sometimes people can be a week late especially if they are sending in cheques, but serious rent arrears are not that common. Check also to see if there is a guarantor on the contract. If there is, do not hesitate to write or ring the guarantor, tell them the tenant has not paid, and could they (the guarantor) make a prompt payment to put the matter straight.

It is their responsibility to do so. It's another good argument for having a guarantor on the contract in the first place. Often when you approach a guarantor about problems it inspires them into kicking the tenant into action. A guarantor can be a heck of a sight ruder to a tenant than your could ever be!

You need to keep a close eye on all the rents coming in, another reason why standing orders and computerised banking are so desirable. You can immediately see whether the rents are in or not when you run your daily check. If it isn't, ring the tenant and politely ask if there is a problem with the SOM. Ask them to check with the bank and call you back. Sometimes banks won't make a standing order payment for £500 if there is only £480 in the account. Ask the tenant to bring the full rent to your office as soon as possible to put the matter right.

If another week goes by and the tenant has not corrected the situation it is time for a letter along the lines of, "the rent is overdue and you have not called in to see us or rung back. Please put the matter right within 7 days, otherwise your tenancy could be at risk".

It always pays dividends to be quite strict with new tenants because it establishes a precedent. If you adopt the opposite line, being lenient with newcomers, they might read it that you are being weak. If they do that, things could go downhill quickly.

I have never met a tenant yet who wanted to be evicted and that is the ultimate sanction if they fail to put matters right. Even the merest hint of an eviction rapidly corrects matters in most cases.

Remember, the beauty of an Assured Shorthold Tenancy is that providing the paperwork has been correctly prepared the court is bound to issue an eviction notice once the tenant has missed two monthly payment dates. If you have a tenant who does not pay, you must keep on at them until the matter is resolved. Don't put it to the back of jobs to do, don't ignore it, treat it as your number one priority, and sort it out. Your landlord will appreciate your efforts. They certainly won't, if you leave the matter unresolved.

If the tenant still does not pay, issue them with a notice requiring possession of the property. You can obtain those from Oyez or find them within any management program. It's a very rare hard faced tenant who ignores such an order. If the guarantor doesn't pay, threaten them with legal action as well. It's amazing the quick results a solicitor's letter often produces, and they don't cost a fortune.

If the tenant can't or won't co-operate you will need to go to court and obtain an eviction order. This is very rare believe me, and it is the last thing you want either, as it is both costly and time consuming. In ten years I only went to court twice, and on both occasions the tenant left before the eviction notice could be issued. Speak to your local court office for advice. They are very helpful and will provide you with the necessary forms to complete, and a free booklet explaining the procedure.

It is not unduly complicated and the court office will always help you to get it right. You don't need to employ a solicitor to do this for you. Simply follow the clear instructions laid out on the forms.

4: DAMAGE TO PROPERTY

Dealing with the destroyer tenant depends upon how you discovered the damage. You may have noticed problems during a periodic inspection. In that case you should immediately ask the tenant to put matters right. Follow it up with a letter, that way it is recorded on the file. You can tell them you will return in ten days to inspect the repairs.

If the damage is discovered when you book the tenant out, you can advise them that there will be a deduction from the security deposit to put matters right. The tenant won't like that, but it is their fault and their responsibility. They should have dealt with the matter before the tenancy came to an end. You also have the option of sending a bill to a guarantor, if there is one. You can even invite the guarantor to come and inspect the damage if you feel it would bring matters to a speedy conclusion. Guarantors can and do make good dilapidation bills.

I had one guarantor who coughed up an unbelievable £17,000 for damage that was primarily pet dirt on expensive carpets, rather than face a public court case, and another who paid £4,000 just to bring the matter to a speedy conclusion and to stop us pestering him at work. Always be polite, but be firm, you are only looking to return the property to the condition it was in before the tenant took it. You or the landlord should not be trying to make any additional cash from the incident.

> Guarantors do pay dilapidation bills.
> It is a complete myth they don't.

5: THE MOANER

The complaining tenant is the one I have to confess annoyed me the most. They can become a real pain in the neck. A professional complainer can be on the phone every other day, yes as often as that. The water doesn't heat up quickly enough, the garage needs painting, the television reception is poor, the gutters could do with a clean, one of the tiles on the kitchen floor is cracked, and the tree needs pruning, etc, etc, etc. The list is endless. You name it and the real complainer can moan about it.

Don't get me wrong; if there is a genuine maintenance problem, it has to be dealt with as soon as possible, full stop. But there are genuine problems and spurious ones and the professional moaner doesn't seem capable of seeing the difference. You might consider a quiet word in the tenant's ear along the lines of, "your tenancy is soon to be renewed isn't it, and we don't really want to bother the landlord over that do we?" This often works wonders, and unfortunately sometimes it is your only option. Use your best judgement. Some people are never satisfied and they will test your patience to the limit, and beyond. It wastes your time, and distracts you from your prime aims.

Personally, if a tenant were continually unreasonable I would recommend to the landlord that the tenancy agreement was not renewed. They could always move out and take a tenancy in one of your competitor's properties. Let your rivals have the hassle. There are plenty of other fishes in the sea, and good ones too.

6: The NON-MOVER

Lastly, Barnacle Bill, the one who downs anchors and refuses to budge. This is the nightmare scenario that landlords always imagine will happen to them. I cannot emphasise enough how rare this is. The ultimate sanction would be for Barnacle and his family of little urchins to be visited by bailiffs and ultimately be forcibly removed from the home and dumped in the rain on the lawn together with their belongings.

The tenant knows that will be the final outcome, and they'd have to be either very stupid or disturbed to follow that route. Believe me, I come back once again to the referencing at the outset; if you have done your job properly, it should never happen.

If it does, get an eviction order, the tenant only has himself to blame. If they won't move out under their own steam, recruit the full force of the law to remove them. They will be evicted. It's as simple as that.

Tenants who don't pay the rent &
Tenants who don't look after the property
are NOT wanted.
Move them on, let your competitors enjoy them
and find someone else.

BAD CUSTOMERS:

All businesses have the occasional bad customer, for that is what the tenant's are, your, and your landlord's customers. What matters is how you deal with them. To do nothing and hope that things will be all right, is a very bad policy. If you have a problem, confront it as early as you can, and sort it.

But when you do have a problem with a tenant, it is advisable to keep your landlord fully informed of the difficulty at the earliest opportunity. It is not an easy phone call to make, but it is an important one. The odds are they will understand, they have probably had difficulties themselves in the past. Hopefully they'll simply tell you to: "get on with it and sort it out. You're the agent aren't you?"

If you leave it for weeks without mentioning a problem to a landlord, it becomes harder and harder to tell them, and when you eventually do, they have the killer question back, "You've known about this for seven weeks and you haven't told me anything about it. Why the heck not?" They won't be happy, and your relationship could become strained. (Or worse!)

Establish a clear procedure
for dealing with difficult tenants.
Confront problems head on
Put warnings in writing
Keep Landlords Informed.

THINGS YOU MUST NOT DO:

When you do have problems with a tenant there are some things you must never do. You can visit the house to discuss the matter, but you mustn't visit the house threatening people, and you must never employ others to threaten or intimidate. You must never interfere with the supply of services to the house. You must not enter the house and change the locks, and you must not lock the tenant out.

The courts take a very dim view of intimidation, threatening behaviour, and harassment, and rightly so. If you adopt policies such as those, you shift your position from being 100% in the right, with the full force of the law behind you, to being outside the law, and at risk from prosecution yourself. There are ways and means of doing things. Never cross the line into illegality.

Make sure that at all times you operate in the correct manner. Bear in mind that if the matter came to court you could be cross-examined, and you do not want to be in the position of admitting any illegal activities or moves.

Never be bullied by over zealous landlords into breaking the law. Some will try to push you, you can be sure of that. If you have any doubts as to what you are doing, speak to your solicitor IMMEDIATELY.

Get to know the law
Stay within the law
Use the law when necessary
Solve problems out of court
Courts cost time and money.

Chapter 20:   Extending Contracts and Inspecting Properties

An Assured Shorthold Tenancy agreement should be for a minimum of three months but the usual minimum period is for six months. But you can if you wish prepare a contract for two years or even longer. I would not recommend a contract for longer than two years because you are tying the landlord into a fixed rental they cannot then increase. Imagine if rampant inflation returned, and who says it couldn't?

Everything would go up, except the landlord's rental figure. There's another reason too for avoiding longer tenancies and that's included in the section on stamp duty.

LIASE WITH BOTH PARTIES:

It's a good idea to regularly liase with both the tenant and landlord to discover their thinking with regard to extending contracts. Many tenants will openly tell you if they are planning to leave after six months, or alternatively that they would like to remain in the house for another year, or longer. A good agent always knows what their tenant's are looking for.

When an initial period expires the tenancy does NOT come to an automatic end, unless the appropriate notice bringing it to an end has been served or the tenant has confirmed in writing they wish to leave. If no notice has been served, the tenancy relapses to what is called a Periodic Tenancy.

This Periodic contract runs on indefinitely until one party or the other brings it to a close. The landlord, or agent would need to serve the appropriate notice, which would give the tenant a minimum of two month's notice that the landlord required possession of the property.

On the other side of the coin, you should note that the tenant would only have to give one month's notice IN WRITING, to bring the contract to a close. Either party cannot give notice over the telephone. If a tenant rings the office and says, "I'm giving a month's notice", you must ask them to confirm the fact in writing. If you don't have a letter, you have no proof the tenant gave notice, and it wouldn't be the first tenant who changed their mind or told a fib and denied all knowledge of the telephone conversation.

ISSUING A NOTICE REQUIRING POSSESSION:

So it follows that if the landlord wishes possession of the property at the end of the six months you MUST issue the appropriate notice after 4 months, in effect giving the tenant 2 month's notice. It's a good idea to do that 7 or 14 day's prior to the cut off point. It's also a good idea to hand the notice in person to the tenant, or send it by recorded delivery, so you are certain it has been delivered.

Why not write on the file when you start any let a date when you know notice needs to be given? If you flip through the files every week you will keep abreast of which tenancies are approaching the cut-off point. Or better still diarise the fact so you don't forget, then liase with the landlord. Good agents always have an idea of their landlords and tenants thinking regarding the period beyond the tenancy, for ALL their lets.

A FURTHER FIXED TERM:

Once the initial contract is approaching an end, and is due to revert to a Periodic Tenancy the landlord may feel uneasy that the tenant could give a month's notice and quit. The way around that is to issue a Memorandum extending the existing contract for a further fixed term. You do not need to prepare a whole new tenancy agreement.

Bear in mind it's in your interest too. If you have a satisfactory letting proceeding without any problems at say £750 per month, you could be retaining £75 of that. or more per month. If you can extend the contract for another year you are locking in another £900 guaranteed minimum revenue for yourself.

If the property became empty, anything might happen. The landlord might give the house to another agent for one, he could sell it for another, or move into it himself, or give it to his son or daughter, or you might struggle to let it again. These are all incentives for you, and the landlord, if rental income is paramount, to keep the tenant in the property, and the best way to do that is to have both parties sign an extension.

The Memorandum should simply refer to the original tenancy agreement, listing the start date, and the parties involved. It should state, "The tenancy has been extended for a further 6 months (or whatever figure you like, up to 24) and will now end on June 26th 2006 (or whatever date). All other terms and conditions remain unchanged."

You could also consider a rent increase too at this time, providing you don't frighten the tenant away. If an increase is agreed simply incorporate that fact in the Memo. Remember too, to amend any standing order mandates if you bump up the rent. Prepare the Memo in duplicate, have both parties sign, and send a signed copy to each party. Take a photocopy too and stick it in your file and remember to diarise it again for when the contract is next due to be renewed or reviewed.

CHARGING FOR EXTENSIONS:

Some agents charge for this service, others don't, relying on the fact they have locked in the existing contract for another fixed term in the sure knowledge they have protected their revenue for another year or so. We charged a small fee, £40, and as long as it was listed in your original Fact Pack, you are quite within your rights to charge for the service if you so wish. If you do, you've created another revenue stream for yourself. That's what it's all about. Creating revenue, because creating revenue gives you power.

PROPERTY INSPECTIONS:

Inspecting properties during the tenant's stay is an important duty you should carry out. Some landlords absolutely insist on regular inspections of all their properties, especially the more nervous ones, but some landlords don't give a hoot whether you inspect or not. Indeed there is an argument that says that too frequent inspections may unsettle a good tenant and they may up sticks and move away.

Neither you nor your landlord can just roll up at the property without notice and demand to be let in to carry out an on the spot inspection. The contract states that the tenant should "enjoy quiet enjoyment" of the property and obviously an on the spot unannounced inspection is not within the spirit of the let.

When an inspection is due, write to the tenant and say: "under the terms of the tenancy we are required to carry out an inspection of the property and we intend to do this at 10am next Thursday. If this is not a convenient time please ring our office and arrange an alternative appointment".

I would always give a tenant between five and seven days notice before the appointment. We can all be untidy at times, and how would you like people turning up with little or no notice to inspect your house? I know I wouldn't.

Additionally if the tenant has broken or damaged something, it gives them the opportunity to fix it before you arrive. The chances are they will ring up, whether they want to change the date or not. Usually they simply ask what's it all about? All you need answer is that you are obliged to check things over to make sure everything is all right. You can reassure them it is normal practice and that it won't take very long.

INSPECTING PROPERTIES:

On the day of the inspection arrive at the house on time and be cheerful. Try not to act like the hated teacher at school who crept round the class trying to find fault with everything he could. Make notes as you go round and if there is anything you see that needs dealing with, you can mention it there and then if you wish.

Children's writing on walls is a common complaint, new stains on the carpets, anything that catches your eye, you have the opportunity to point it out to the tenant and hint that they need to sort it. Remember, if they don't do anything to correct the situation they may be hit in the pocket via a claim against the deposit when the tenancy comes to a close.

Inspect every room, and outside the property too. Has the lawn been cut? That is the tenant's responsibility. If they haven't done so, it will need to be done. If you don't feel comfortable asking the tenant to carry out certain tasks there and then, you can return to the office and write them a polite letter pointing out your findings and asking them to put the matters right.

In my experience it is preferable to have a friendly chat and point things out while you are there, than write a letter a few days later. No matter how well worded the letter may be, sometimes the tone may sound harsh and confrontational. Remember, you are not aiming to upset the tenant; you are simply endeavouring to ensure that the tenancy is being conducted in a satisfactory manner for all parties.

Indeed the tenant may well take the opportunity to point out various maintenance jobs that need addressing that are possibly the landlord's responsibility. Perhaps some guttering is leaking, or a fence has blown down. When you return to the office, prepare your report as soon as possible while it is fresh in the memory, keep a copy on file as proof you have carried out an inspection, and mail the original to the landlord. DO NOT send a copy to the tenant.

Problems solved during routine inspections often go a long way to eradicating difficulties that may arise at the end of the tenancy, so treat it seriously and prepare the ground for a trouble free end to that particular let.

If the landlord has been unaware of the impending inspection they may well be pleased to receive your report out of the blue. It will reinforce in their mind how well you are doing your job, which you are. They may also discuss with you carrying our maintenance jobs as recommended by your good selves and that could mean additional possible revenue, so it hasn't been a complete waste of time, financially speaking. It is in everyone's ultimate interest that all properties are maintained to a high standard.

HOW OFTEN SHOULD INSPECTIONS BE CARRIED OUT?

That's a difficult question to answer. As previously mentioned some landlords don't care about inspections at all. It may seem strange, but it's true. Others would have an inspection carried out every week, if they could! You will have discussed with your landlords their thoughts on the matter. Some tenants need to be inspected more regularly than others, some very rarely, others regularly, and you will soon become an expert at deciding which. Some tenants will do everything they can to stop you inspecting the property too. In that case you should ask yourself, why?

If that occurs you should persist in your request for a suitable appointment. If a tenant consistently puts you off you might consider calling at the house unannounced. If the tenant is in they might let you in, but more likely they will give you an appointment to call back later. You can point out that under the terms of the agreement they are bound to grant you access. They are breaking the terms of the contract if they consistently deny you entry.

As previously mentioned neither you nor your landlord may enter the property at anytime without the tenant being present unless you have the tenant's clear permission to do so, or a court order. Some landlords, especially the amateurs find this very difficult to adhere to. They might say, "this was my late mother's house and I'll go in and check whenever I like". But they can't.

Never be railroaded into entering a house with a landlord unless you have extraordinarily good reasons to do so. For example, if you thought the tenant was seriously ill. You always need a valid reason to enter, and to be on the safe side it might be an idea to ask a policeman to accompany you.

ENTERING HOUSES WITHOUT PERMISSION:

I had one landlord who couldn't stop himself entering his property in the afternoon. One day the tenant came home early and found him standing there in the middle of the sitting room.

"What the hell are you doing here?" Shouted the furious woman.
"I just thought I'd let myself in, to see that everything was all right."
"Oh did you? Well take that!" The tenant was so livid; she slapped him hard about the face and hustled him from the building.

She rang me up in a fury and refused from that point onward to pay any further rental until she received a written apology and an assurance that no one would enter the house again without her knowledge. The fact is, the landlord could have been there to steal the tenant's possessions, he wasn't, but he could have been.

Some landlords need guidance and expertise. Many things are a matter of common sense. Remember, once the landlord signs that tenancy agreement he no longer has the same rights and uses over the property as he had before. That is precisely what the tenant is paying for, so if you ever feel that the landlord is overstepping the mark; don't be afraid to politely point out the dangers. In the longer term they'll thank you for it, or at least they should do.

Be aware of your tenant's and landlord's thinking
Before tenancy agreements expire
Carry out Inspections as required
Do not enter properties without the tenant's permission, or a Court Order

Chapter 21: Booking Tenants Out

As the end of the tenancy approaches ring the tenant and make an appointment to meet them at the property when they will hopefully have removed all their belongings from the house. With regard to removal arrangements, you will need to remain somewhat flexible regarding the time, as removal companies, or departing tenants, don't always finish when they say they will.

When you speak to the tenant impress upon them how important it is that the property should be returned in the same condition it was let when they moved in. (Allowing for fair wear and tear.)

Remind the tenant that the house should be thoroughly cleaned, especially if pets have been in the property. You can also politely point out that should the property not be returned in the same neat and tidy condition, the landlord could seek an allowance from the deposit to cover cleaning costs and make good any damage.

TASKS TO BE COMPLETED ON BOOKING OUT DAY:

When you attend the property you will need to carry out the following duties:

- Inspect for any damage, if there is any, note it, and point it out to the tenant
- Note down the meter readings

189

- Check the inventory for missing or damaged contents
- Note down the tenant's forwarding address to send back any the deposit
- Advise the utility companies where to post their final bills
- Collect ALL the keys issued to the tenant
- Remind the tenant to arrange for the forwarding of their mail
- Let the tenant out of the house, and lock the door behind them. The tenant should NOT re-enter the property again at any time thereafter without your permission
- Place a to-let sign, if you have been instructed to let the property again, in the front window with the telephone number clearly visible
- Remind the tenant to cancel the standing order mandate. You cannot do it for them, and it's surprising how many people forget

RETURNING TENANT'S DEPOSITS:

Some tenants will try and hassle you to give them back their deposit there and then, and in cash too. Don't be browbeaten into agreeing anything of the sort. Remind them of the clear clause on their application form that we mentioned early, "The deposit will be returned by cheque within 14 days to your new address providing the rent account is up to date and the property is returned in the same condition".

You, as the agent, always abide by the terms of the contract, and it is not too much to expect tenants to do the same.

This is a very important and powerful clause because it reinforces the point that the new address given to you by the tenant will be their correct forwarding address. It is unlikely they would want a cheque going to a bogus address.

Tenants will sometimes come up with all sorts of reasons as to why they can't adhere to this clause, and if they do, you should ask yourself why? Could it be that something is amiss?

Return to the office and write to the utility companies, as you did when you introduced the tenant. This time of course you are advising them that the tenant has been booked out, that their new address is such and such and that the closing meter reading was XXXXXXX. The utility companies will then send their final bills for that tenant to the new address.

ADVISE THE LANDLORD THE TENANT HAS VACATED:

Telephone the landlord and advise them that the property has been successfully recovered. Discuss with them the state of the property. If you deem the house to be in good order and the landlord agrees, return the deposit to the tenant as soon as possible.

It is good PR to return deposits quickly to tenants where they have clearly returned the property in good order. Why? Because they will certainly rent from you again when they are next looking for rented accommodation. Many tenants often return as renters time after time. They might also recommend you to other potential tenants. Word of mouth recommendation by tenants is almost as good as by landlords.

There are many agencies (and landlords too) who have a reputation for almost never returning deposits, or at least fighting for the very last pound before doing so. Yes, they might gain some additional cash in the short term but in my view this is a very shortsighted policy.

You are in this business for the long haul and there is nothing to be gained from being unnecessarily confrontational, unless you simply enjoy rows! Even if you are building up the business purely to sell on at a later date, you don't want to be handing over a business that no one ever has a good word to say about. Think "goodwill" not "badwill". No one will want to buy a business weighed down with years of sour and mean baggage when it comes to your exit strategy.

Some landlords will want to inspect the properties themselves prior to the deposit being returned, and that's their prerogative.

PROCESSING DILAPIDATION CLAIMS:

If there is a claim for damage, for example a toilet seat is broken and missing, you can make a deduction from the deposit and return the balance to the tenant together with a letter stating why there has been a deduction. A receipt for a new toilet seat would prove the expense incurred.

It has to be said there are some landlords who try and get their hands on the deposit purely as an additional form of revenue with spurious and exaggerated claims.

This must be resisted. Yes, the landlord employs you, but you are not retained to lie on their behalf. If there is a justified claim, then deduct the money. If there is not, you cannot become involved in deducting money unjustifiably. If you do, you may find the tenant commences legal action against both you and the landlord. The courts do not look kindly on landlords and agents who are seen to be trying to exploit tenants in this way. Fair and reasonable are words that spring to mind.

DILAPIDATION DISPUTES:

If a mutual agreement cannot be reached over a claim, an independent arbitrator may need to be appointed. You won't be surprised to learn that independent arbitrators have to be paid for. The result? Everyone loses. Avoid it happening by encouraging all parties to settle amicably.

Occasionally you will lose a landlord because you have not followed their wishes to the letter, and so be it. Your conscience is quite clear if you have done everything by the book. It is better to lose the occasional landlord, than be dragged through the courts, over what you judge to be a spurious claim. Remember, the last thing you want is a lurid article in the local press along the lines of:

BRENTS RENTS SUED OVER WITHHOLDING DEPOSITS
AGENT FINED £5,000, and warned as to future conduct.

That is a nightmare scenario never to be contemplated. The vast majority of landlords are fair and reasonable people, just like you and me, most simply want their monthly rental payment in order they can pay their mortgages or maintain their Spanish villas. Advise landlords they could face court action if they persist with an unjustifiable claim. Remember too, the best way to take the landlord's mind off claiming a few quid for a missing set of cheap tumblers is to let the property again as quickly as possible.

And another thing. When it comes to dilapidation disputes it isn't unusual in the heat of the moment for tempers to become frayed, and occasionally people say things they might later regret. Often the next day, after a good night's sleep (or a sleepless night!) things appear totally different.

Try not to let these issues cloud your thinking. There is little point in wasting a lot of time and brainpower over a missing washing up bowl worth 99p, when you should be concentrating on how and when you are going to re-let the property.

DON'T LEAVE PROPERTIES EMPTY:

Bear in mind that the longer any property remains empty, the more likely it is the landlord will instruct another agent to let it, and consequently, the more likely it is, that you will lose it. Property Instructions to any letting agent are their life-blood. The last thing you want to do is lose the house to BONE'S HOMES up on the hill. Any house.

You should be letting them too, long before the competition, because you had more than a head's start over them. To begin with you knew the property was coming empty long before they did, and you should have been advertising and promoting it for at least three weeks before you finally took possession.

Any good agent would already have someone lined up for it. You are a good agent, because you are always thinking ahead. Once you have a good property on your books you must do everything in your power to keep it. If you keep the landlord sweet it is not unusual to retain a house for ten or fifteen years. Plenty of retained properties produces plenty of profit, for you.

When a house comes empty and you lose it to one of your rivals, you should ask yourself why it happened. And more than that, you should redouble your efforts to make sure it doesn't happen again. Try and take one back off them if you can, even up the score. How does that phrase go? Don't get angry – get even!

THE CHANGEOVER CAN BE A STRESSFUL TIME:

The whole process of moving house and booking tenants in and out of properties can be a stressful business. It's quite a complicated affair and all sorts of things can and do go wrong.

It might bucket down with rain all day, the removal men could be late, the tenant might not arrive, or may not be ready to move out, the electricity or gas might not be on (as was arranged), an essential repair that a potential tenant previously pointed out, might not have been carried out, despite you arranging for it to be done.

No matter what the difficulty is, the secret is to keep calm, remain cheerful and positive. Don't lose your temper, always remain helpful and seemingly in control. Don't become tetchy and agitated, leave that for others, and no matter how much you may dislike a particular individual, don't let it become personal. Treat everyone with your same professional manner and you will be fine.

Landlords occasionally attend the move day, even though they have employed you to look after such matters, and unfortunately some of them can't resist making the changeover more difficult than it might otherwise be. Sometimes they become incredibly tense and that is all the more reason that you remain calm and in control. That very tenseness is contagious. Cool heads always deal with matters better than hot heads. It seems so simple and straight forward doesn't it? It makes you wonder why everyone doesn't see matters in the same light. Unfortunately they don't.

Remind yourself if necessary that your main goal is to return to the office as soon as possible and concentrate on letting not just that house, but other properties too. Booking tenants out is a necessary chore, but don't let it take more of your thinking time than is absolutely necessary.

Remain calm. Remain helpful
Rise above tensions
Get the job done. Get away!

Chapter 22: Tax, Tax, and Tax Again

The taxman! What a subject! Don't we all just love the guy? When you first start DENT'S RENTS you should tell the Inland Revenue that you have commenced in the lettings business as an agent. You are obliged to do so, and should do so, after all it's not as if they can send you a tax bill when you first start your business.

It may be tempting not to bother, but sooner or later they will become aware of your activities and they will be miffed if you haven't advised them. Start as you mean to go on, and tell them where you are, and what you are doing.

THE VATMAN:

You have no need to register for VAT until your turnover rises above £60,000 per annum (at the time of writing. Your local VAT office will confirm if that figure has changed.) But keep a careful eye on your turnover figure as it rises, because sooner or later you will approach and bust that figure, and the VATMAN takes no prisoners when they discover traders who have exceeded the threshold and are still unregistered.

I made that mistake and when the VAT inspector came and looked through our books he was able to show that we had exceeded the threshold by a measly £180 ten months before we actually thought we had. This resulted in us receiving a VAT claim for the missing ten months for all the VAT that we <u>should</u> have charged to our clients on our fees.

We couldn't pass on those additional costs retrospectively for work done months before. Technically we might have done, but it would have been such a PR nightmare we bit our tongue and stood the bill. I thought the VAT office were being particularly mean but all the guy could say as he smiled was: "it's nothing personal, pity really!" Yeah it was that. We'd made a silly mistake, albeit an honest one, and paid for it. Make sure you don't.

Someone told me VAT inspectors are paid commission on any additional VAT they can dig up. I don't know if that's true and I'm sure they'd deny it, but if it is, I think it should be stopped, because it makes them over zealous.

The TAX communities are the one institution who do not have to prove you guilty of an offence. In any tax investigation you have to prove yourself innocent. This is incredibly difficult to do. If the taxman says: "I think you have drawn £2,000 out of that business you have not declared", how the heck do you prove you otherwise?

So make sure you register for VAT in good time. Incidentally at the time of writing residential rents are not subject to VAT, although I wonder how long that will remain the case. If there is no necessity to charge VAT on rents, your agency fees are vatable, so you will need to charge your clients VAT once you have broken through the threshold.

On a £1,000 per month let, where you are taking 10% commission, your monthly fee of £100 would then be subject to VAT. Assuming the rate is 17.5%, the VAT chargeable and subsequently payable to the VAT office would be £17.50. So it follows that where the landlord was suffering a £100 monthly deduction from his rent before you were registered for VAT, the total deduction would increase to £117.50 after you have registered. You can clearly see from that example why landlords will love to deal with you before you are registered. They receive more money; it's as simple as that. If in any doubt, consult your accountant who will clarify all VAT matters for you.

OVERSEAS LANDLORDS TAX LIABILITY:

The third taxman you will need to keep a close eye upon involves overseas landlords. You might think it would be unusual to have an overseas landlord, but with so many Britons now living abroad, especially in France, Greece, Spain and Portugal, not to mention the United States, overseas landlords are becoming very common.

The important point to bear in mind here is that unless you have an approval number from the local Inland Revenue Overseas Residents Department to pay the rental in full to the landlord, you as the agent will become liable for tax on that income. If you don't have an approval number you should deduct 23% (this rate fluctuates with tax rates, and it might be an idea to check the rate with the Overseas Residents Department) from the rental and retain it ready for paying over to the Revenue. They will send you an annual or quarterly returns form, which on completion shows the total rental collected, and the total tax that YOU, as the responsible collecting agent, must pay to the Revenue.

Of course you are being used again as an unpaid tax collector, and we all know there is nothing new in that and nothing you can do about it. If you sent a bill to the Chancellor's office for the time you spent on it, I think we'd all know the outcome of that. If you have an approval number for each landlord, you simply list that number and the matter is closed. You can then pay the landlord his rent in full, after fees.

If you paid all the rent money, say £8,000 in a given year without making tax deductions, to an owner who is basking in the Greek sunshine, and the Revenue then asked you to pay 23% of it back to them, you wouldn't be very happy. In my experience the vast majority of landlords receive an approval number without any difficulty and most overseas residents who rent out property are well aware of this arrangement.

It won't come as a nasty surprise to most of them, but don't let them browbeat you into releasing all of the cash by saying, "it'll be all right, if there's a problem at a later date I can always reimburse you". You are obliged to deduct the tax at source if you haven't a number, and that is all there is to it.

Perhaps the landlord already knows they are not entitled to an approval number, in which case you will be landed with the bill. Without an approval number it won't be, "all right". Don't fall into this chasm of a mistake. Get it right from the beginning, and you will have a stress free life when it comes to overseas landlord's tax. You might even earn a few pounds of interest as the deducted money for the taxman remains on deposit in your client's bank account, until the payment to the Revenue office becomes due.

LIASE WITH THE REVENUE:

Speak to your local Inland Revenue office; they will put you through to the right department. Ask them to send you the relevant booklets and forms to apply for approval numbers. It is not a huge tome like some of the stuff they send out. It's simply written and easy to follow, and if you still have a problem with it, ring them up and ask for assistance and advice. You may be pleasantly surprised how eager they are to help. They'll supply you with all the free pamphlets that you can hand to your overseas landlords from the outset. You could even incorporate them into your Fact Pack.

Should one of your existing landlords suddenly move abroad you would also need to start making that 23% deduction immediately, until an approval number is issued. No approval number means, No full rental payment to the overseas landlord, full stop. Remember, the Revenue Office will always ask you to pay over this money, regardless of whether you have deducted it or not, and they will not accept any excuses, particularly along the lines of "I've only just started in business and I didn't know". Ignorance of the law is no defence. Don't be caught out.

Valued Added Tax:
Don't Forget to Register in Time

Your Fees are Vatable
Residential Rents are Not

The Threshold Figure Changes
Keep Aware of it

Overseas Landlords Rent is Taxable
Unless you have an Approval Number
The Agent is Responsible for Retaining and Paying
That Tax to the Revenue

Chapter 23: I Don't Want to be an Estate Agent!

Well of course you don't, after all aren't estate agents consistently ranked alongside traffic wardens as the profession the general public most love to hate? (An unjustifiable reputation, in my humble opinion, as almost all the estate agents I have ever known have been very hard working and conscientious).

But as you become a more established and successful letting and management agent I guarantee that you will start to glance enviously at your estate agent cousins. Why? Money of course. If an estate agent sells a single property worth £300,000 even on the lower bands of 1% commission, that agent would earn at least £3,000. It takes a large number of lets and hard work to earn £3,000 in letting revenue.

Contrary to the popular view I don't think an estate agent does more work on a single transaction than a letting agent. Do they have to read meters, write to services, check inventories, reference tenants, prepare a legal tenancy agreement, and collect deposits? No, they don't, most don't even bother to accompany viewers. So I guess it's natural that a letting agent should look at the estate agent's large commission with more than simply an envious eye.

 CONSIDERING ESTATE AGENCY:

Even if you have no intention of ever becoming an estate agent, I can guarantee certain circumstances will arise that will at the very least make you think more about it.

The property letting and management business like so many industries runs in cycles. Some months you will be rushed off your feet, other periods you will suddenly find time on your hands.

January and September are invariably busy months for lettings, the children have gone back to school, and many employed people are starting new jobs and new employment contracts, often away from their hometowns. Many of these people decide to retain their own homes and rent a second property to be nearer their new workplace.

The property letting business can also be affected by changing house prices. When prices are low and depressed and sales are slow moving, a great deal more property floods on to the lettings market. Perhaps some landlords and property owners suddenly have negative equity, where even if they wanted to sell, they are debarred from doing so, unless they are prepared to make good the shortfall in equity.

Perhaps sales are not moving and to avoid the property standing empty, many property owners will turn to the lettings market, and rent out for a short time to cover their mortgage payments. They'll do this until prices and demand picks up again. This can be a very successful time for letting agents because there will be an almost unlimited number of properties available to be let out. Grab them while they're there, as many as you can, and lock them into decent length contracts which protects your forward income.

THE MONDAY MORNING CALLS:

But when property prices move up sharply, some of these landlords will, possibly for the first time, see the opportunity to bale out, to take a fat juicy profit, and many will do just that. Horribly they often come together in batches of five and six houses at a time, and usually from completely unconnected landlords and when you least expect it. You experience the rush of those Monday morning telephone calls along the lines of: "I've been thinking over the weekend". You wonder what's coming, and then they hit you.

Your friendly landlord, the same person for whom you have worked so hard to please, and who, you could be forgiven for thinking would remain with you for years to come, suddenly tells you they have grown tired of letting, and are selling up. Oh dear! Sometimes they will cursorily add: "You don't do sales do you?"

You confirm the fact, you don't do sales, and the next thing you know, your four fine much coveted houses suddenly appear in the much-maligned Snodgrass and Company's fine advertisement, FOR SALE. You glance at the asking prices, £150,000, £200,000, £250,000 and £300,000 and you snort and think, they'll never sell them at those prices! He's wasting his time!

But suddenly the market's moving up, the buyer's are back in droves, and within three weeks all four houses have incredibly sold. They will never appear on the rental market ever again, and you curse aloud. Your mind goes into overdrive, and you begin to think about that commission, that money, and about how you could increase YOUR fees.

You work out in your mind that those four houses sold for the thick end of £900,000 and even on just 1% commission old Snodgrass has just trousered nine grand, for three week's work! Nine grand! That's a heck of a lot of rental commissions. How many houses would you have to rent, and how long would those contracts have to run, to make nine grand? A single house earning you £50 per month commission would have to be rented out for fifteen years to make nine flipping grand! And he's pocketed it, this week!

And worse still than that, old Snodgrass has twenty more to come, judging by his ever-growing advertisement of colourful properties for sale, and you think, Heck! What is going on here? What is to stop me SELLING HOUSES TOO? The answer is: NOTHING! ABSOLUTELY NOTHING!

NO LICENCE IS REQUIRED:

At the time of writing you do not need a licence to set up an estate agency business in England and Wales. You cannot do so if you have been made bankrupt, or if the Office of Fair Trading informs you that you must not. They might take that course of action if they hold numerous complaints on their files about the way you have conducted your business affairs in the past, another good reason to run a straight and honest enterprise.

Other than that, you can, but you MUST be fully aware that the legalities of trading as an estate agency are entirely different to that of being a letting agent.

For a start you have to rigidly comply with the Trade Descriptions Act of 1968 but much more importantly with the Estate Agency Act of 1979 and most especially the Property Misdescriptions Act of 1991. To fail to do so could land you in serious and expensive trouble. Check out the web site www. oft.gov.uk and look at the section dealing with estate agency. Here are just three simple examples of where you could run into trouble.

Firstly, if you included room measurements on your property particulars and were just six inches out, you could be prosecuted by the Office of Fair Trading or indeed by a potential property buyer, even if it was a genuine typing error by your new young typist. An accidental mistake is no defence. Fines can run into huge figures. Best to get professional indemnity insurance, believe me. You could even be de-barred from trading overnight. Not a happy thought.

Secondly, if you sell a property you own, or one belonging to a relative, you are legally obliged to include that fact prominently within the sales particulars. If you didn't, the same penalties could be imposed.

Thirdly, if you displayed a property in the window at £200,000 but inside your shop, or office, or in one of your advertisements you had reduced it to £190,000 and had forgotten to amend your window display, you could once again be falling foul of the Acts and could face surprisingly severe penalties. I am not trying to put you off the idea, but rather to steer you well clear of the many slippery crevasses that lie strewn across your path.

If you are interested in developing your business into estate agency, study the ramifications of the Acts, speak to your trade associations, check out the myriad of information that is available on the internet, teach yourself all there is to know, and ultimately you will be well equipped to set up your own sales division. And the next time there's a rush of properties leaving the rental sector and a landlord says to you, "You don't do sales do you?" You can reply smiling, "But of course we do, we'll get right on it."

NO ONE IS BETTER PLACED TO START:

You are in an excellent position to do so too, because you have a register of landlords just waiting for your attention. You could mail shot them all, something along the lines of:

THINKING OF SELLING? – LOOK NO FURTHER!

You could offer a special deal to your long-term clients, and don't forget too, that you may well have professional clients and landlords looking to BUY property, to expand their own property portfolios.

Try and match them, to produce quick sales, at low cost to yourself. You could pocket the commission for selling a property; yet still have the opportunity to rent it out for the new owners. What could be better? Use your imagination, the potential is limitless.

YOU DON'T NEED A SHOP:

Contrary to popular opinion, you don't need a shop to sell property. Many real estate agents in the USA don't have a shop, they carry out their entire operation from office-based accommodation, and there are many more businesses doing precisely the same thing here. It is becoming quite common. A display advertisement with a good photograph in your local newspaper is your shop window, along with the Internet of course, and that's all you need.

The only person who won't appreciate your new enterprise is old Snodgrass of course, and you don't owe him a living. Would he help you out with additional rental properties when your market was quiet? Fat chance!

Here's another thought too. During the past five or six years a huge number of new independent estate agencies have opened up from Tenerife to Tottenham, from Miami to Manchester and seemingly all stops in between. In recent months with property prices turning slightly downward, quite a few of these new independents have lost a little interest and some have started to sell up and get out of the industry. If house prices continue to be depressed you can expect to see more people looking to cut and run.

Why is that so interesting? Because it produces opportunities, that's why. Some of these people simply want out, some are desperate to get out, and have cut their asking prices to achieve it. If you are serious about looking at estate agency, pick up a copy of Dalton's Weekly. That is the paper that specialises in selling businesses. It comes out every Thursday and in there you will probably find some estate agents for sale, and some of them are now very attractively priced.

I've seen agencies for sale at a figure far less than it would cost to buy a shop lease and refurbish the premises. The beauty of buying an established business is that you not only acquire ready equipped premises, but also a register of properties ready to go. A register of properties equates to early potential income, and combined with what you have already built up yourself, this could give your business a massive boost. In many cases you might not need to take the shop if you don't want to. Occasionally the value of the existing property register is worth more than the asking price alone.

If you are tempted to buy an established business make sure you are not taking on any of their previous, possibly hidden debts, or any VAT liability, or any liability for uncollected rental on properties they may have managed. Again your accountant will advise you on the more intricate details to do with purchasing an ongoing business.

If you are interested in branching into this sector of the property market, and you have the necessary capital to do so, consider acquiring an established business because there is good value to be had when sellers are keen to get out. And when you find something to suit you, remember to haggle aggressively over the price. The sellers are advertising their businesses for sale because they want out, sometimes at almost any price. You as a buyer are giving them that exit strategy, perhaps no one else will, so make sure you strike the best deal you possibly can.

Incidentally, property management and letting does not come under the scope of the Estate Agents Act, but as I have mentioned before it is a very good idea to study and gain a qualification both for lettings and sales. Sooner or later I am sure this will become a statutory requirement. It will also impress your clients and induce confidence in you as a professional person, when they notice you're signing correspondence with the appropriate letters after your name. It's not as hard to achieve as you might imagine.

BUT I DON'T WANT TO BE AN ESTATE AGENT...

Well of course you don't. Protest away. But would you like an additional £20,000 of earnings EVERY MONTH? Yes? Well, might I suggest you are now fully aware of where that could be found? Eight sold properties at £250,000 each on 1% commission would produce that £20,000. It is not impossible, it really isn't.

One last point on this topic. Imagine for a moment if you earned an extra £20,000 per month. That could provide you with the necessary deposit to buy a new property for rental <u>EVERY MONTH</u>. That is twenty-four houses in two years. If each of those houses went up by just £41,667 in those two years, as they probably have in the last two years, you would be sitting on equity of....yes, you've guessed it, a million squid!

Yes, I know I'm playing with figures, and there are squillions of other factors to consider, but it makes you think doesn't it? If it doesn't, it should do.

IF YOU NEED EXTRA CASH?

There would be no tax to pay on that capital gain either, not until you sold the houses, so don't sell. If you ever needed extra cash, go and see your bank manager. Watch his face light up, watch him splutter, when he sees how much equity you have in your portfolio. "You are doing well aren't you? Cash you want, you say? How much would you like? I don't think we've been out for lunch for a little while, have we?"

The potential is there to establish a hugely successful business at relatively low risk, in a comparatively short period of time. You could secure your future for the remainder of your days. So if it's that easy, why don't I do it? Well I did, then sold out, dispatched the business, kept the houses and now I've moved on to other things, (no I didn't make a million, but I'm fine thank you in the folding paper department) and I haven't ruled out the possibility of doing the same thing all over again! One day. So look out – I might just open up near you! Oh, and by the way, it is hard work, but no one has ever said it isn't. But if you are fit and keen, and bright and determined, who's to say you couldn't achieve far more than I ever did.

So what's your excuse? What are you waiting for? You only live once. Are you a dreamer, or a do-er? Even if you achieved only half of what we've imagined, or a quarter, you'd be reasonably happy with that result, wouldn't you?

Chapter 24:   Buying Property

Imagine you have worked incredibly hard and have scrimped and saved enough cash to put down a deposit on your first buy-to-let property. You didn't have any capital to begin with, nor have you been left money by other people, you've had to do it all the hard way, by yourself, off your own back. Now you are ready to buy your first buy-to-let property, but where are you going to buy it?

As we hinted in the previous chapter, the first place to look is within your own business activities.

Ask yourself this: are any of your landlords looking to sell? If they are, ring them up, or better still go and see them, find out what they are thinking. Their properties are almost perfect for you, because you know them so well; they are probably tenanted with first class tenants that you have put into them, and the chances are, they have been well maintained following your regular inspections. But if there isn't anything immediately available within your sphere of influence, or you can't afford them, where do you look after that?

One place you should be extremely careful about becoming involved is via the business opportunity columns in the Sunday newspapers. There has been a huge rise in the number of these companies offering to buy properties (with your money) and manage them for you. What on earth would you need another management agency for? Aren't you by now one of the best agents around?

But, you might say, the properties look so cheap. Yes they do, on the face of it, but they are cheap for a reason, and that reason is probably because no one wants to live in them. Let me ask you a question. Would you buy a car without seeing it? Or a house for you to live in, or even a television set? Without examining it? The answer is obviously no, so why would anyone in their right mind consider buying a house for rental purposes without even seeing it? The answer is, because the proposition looks so good. What is it they say? If a proposition looks too good to be true, it probably is.

The houses that are being touted around are often Victorian and Edwardian terraces that are coming to the end of their natural life. Some of them may even be scheduled to be demolished. Alternatively they are quite likely to be poorly built early 1960's council houses or flats on sprawling estates, many of which contain asbestos, where no one now wants to live, and where the few remaining tenants are desperate to get away from.

Thirdly, they could be modern purpose built flats that are often over-priced to enable a false discount to be built into the asking price. In Lymington in Hampshire a year ago there were apartments being offered for sake at £300,000 where the developer was giving a £15,000 sweetener cheque to buyers who could move in straight away. A year later the sweetener cheques had vanished, but the asking prices on the flats had dropped to £230,000.

There have been a huge number of brand new apartments come on the market in the last eighteen months nationwide, and seemingly bundles more to come, judging by the building going up near me. Some have undeniably been a good buy, but by no means all, and there is some evidence to suggest that the market is becoming saturated with this type of property. There's a block of apartments two miles from me that have been available for nearly three years, and they are still advertising: "last 3 remaining!" They seem to have been saying that since the turn of the century. I saw a survey just last week that suggested a monster 75% of all people who were living in these kind of flats now hankered after switching into a house with a garden where their kids and pets could run around outside, and where they could sit in the sunshine with a glass of wine and read the Sunday papers. I can believe it.

Some buy-to-let owners of these flats have been heading for the exits but to their horror, have found they cannot get the money back they paid for them. The future for fancy buy-to-let apartments in some areas looks difficult at best. The message must be: Be careful!

AND CHEAP PROPERTY CAN ALWAYS GO CHEAPER:

I know of a chap who bought a former council house in Hull for £22,500. He couldn't believe that properties could sell for such a price. On the face of it, it looked a good deal, a reasonably well-built three-bedroom semi detached house with gardens and central heating.

But recently he had it valued by an independent estate agent. The agent said it was now worth £14,500, if he could find a buyer. Remember, no matter how low prices appear, they can always go lower.

That reminds me slightly of the performance of shares in Kingston Communications, also coincidentally based in Hull. I watched closely as their shares tumbled from £15.50 to £5.50. Surely they must be a buy now, I thought, and I bought, big time!

But the shares kept falling, all the way down to 60 pence, where they have bumbled around ever since. Remember, just because prices have fallen, it doesn't mean they can't fall further still.

In addition there have been numerous complaints aired in the newspapers about some of these companies and property clubs, often ironically in the same papers that continue to run these advertisements. The complaints centred on poor property management and poor rental returns. Only last month in Ian Hetherington's column in the Mail on Sunday there was a complaint from a person who bought a house on the promise that rental payments from Housing Benefit would be forthcoming at £325 per month.

In fact payments took an age to start, and when they did they were only £250 per month, thus not even covering the mortgage payment. Clearly the agent wasn't following our advice to collect the shortfall from the tenant. Several of these companies have since closed down. Much money has been lost. Much money has disappeared. These companies are not regulated, though methinks it won't be long before they are. Be warned, do your homework thoroughly.

The properties being touted are often located in what used to be described as depressed areas. Hull, Gateshead, Sunderland, Burnley and Blackburn have all been rich sources for the supply of dirt-cheap housing in recent times. But the north of England in general in the last few years has NOT been a housing black spot when it comes to house values. On the contrary in the past eighteen months, the north of England has seen amongst the largest percentage price rises in the country.

Don't believe me? Well look at this. I bought a three bedroom terraced house in central Birkenhead, an archetypal northern industrial town, for £16,500 in 2000. You won't be surprised to learn that it needed refurbishing. When I'd finished it, it stood me £25,000 all in and it was valued at £36,500. Not a bad return you might think, until you see that last week (June 2005) the house next door, an almost identical property, went on the market for £90,500! And this is in Birkenhead, and anyone who has been there will know that it is not Beverley Hills! Northern industrial towns are not as a whole experiencing poor house prices, so you have to ask yourself again why are the houses that are being touted around still so cheap?

The answer is clear, because no one wants to live in them. The chances are they are located in half empty streets with the windows boarded up. Former council estates now almost completely abandoned to the joy riders and drug dealers who inhabit the streets after dark. If you don't believe me, get in your car, or jump on the train and go and see for yourself.

CHECK LOCATIONS WITH YOUR OWN EYES:

At least that way you will reassure yourself that the properties you are becoming involved with are viable propositions. When you're in the area stay overnight, and drive, or stroll, if you are brave enough, down the streets at ten o' clock at night and really get a feel for the place. If you feel uncomfortable, ill at ease, unsafe even, or intimidated in those areas, then how do you think the potential tenant would feel? Precisely the same I would think.

Northern towns are exactly the same as anywhere else, in that there are many roads that anyone would be happy to live in, and some roads where you definitely would not. If you are buying from your chair a hundred or two hundred miles away, how do you know what sort of streets they are in? You don't! The reason these properties are so cheap, for the most part, is because they are in the roads that nobody else, particularly the locals, want to live in. And if the locals don't want to live there, who in heck's going to rent them?

These run down difficult areas don't even have to be located in northern English towns either. Last year I received details of cheap properties available in Holywell in North Wales. I jumped in the car and drove up there and took a look at them.

I was amazed. The houses were substantial enough semi detached properties, clearly formerly council owned, but in one street alone I counted eight out of the ten houses were boarded up and abandoned. Graffiti covered the boarded windows. A smouldering burnt out car sat half on the pavement and half on the road. A group of obviously bored and unemployed surly youths were lighting cigarettes and were watching my every move.

The former tenants had probably bought them under the council right to buy scheme and at the first available opportunity had fled the neighbourhood to live somewhere nicer. There would have to be an enormous number of improvements to persuade anyone to live in those houses now. I reckon they could easily be bulldozed. They might be dirt-cheap but would you buy them? Would you live there? I doubt it. I wouldn't.

Five minutes drive away were beautiful detached houses selling for £200,000 plus with fantastic views out over the Dee estuary towards the Wirral peninsula. There are streets you'd buy in, and streets you wouldn't. Check out the streets you are buying in yourself, in person, before you buy anything, to do otherwise would be foolish in the extreme.

DEAL DIRECT WITH REPUTABLE ESTATE AGENTS:

If you still believe buying in these areas is a good idea, get hold of the local newspapers and deal directly with a reputable local estate agent. You don't need impressively named property companies to do it for you. They will only charge you a fat fee for the privilege. Established estate agents will give you plenty of free advice as to whether a property will rent or not, and these people are heavily regulated. Is Dick's Property Club subject to the same strict regulation? No. Whatever you do, don't part with any cash to a third party on the back of great promises. You might never see it again.

Some of these clubs and associations charge huge fees, often far more than a long established estate agent, and you have to ask yourself precisely what you are getting for this money. Usually they justify their fees by creating a nominal discount on the asking price. But are these discounts real or imaginary? A good question. I know what I think. What do you think?

My advice would be to concentrate on buying in the areas you know. After all, you have now become a property expert yourself, the biggest property expert in YOUR town, so why would you even consider becoming involved with a company of whom you know little, in a town where you know even less, to purchase a property in a road that could be totally unsellable? It doesn't make a lot of sense does it?

COUNCIL PROPERTY CAN BE GOOD VALUE:

Not all council properties are bad buys, far from it. There are former local authority houses on council estates I wouldn't hesitate to snap up, because I know the estates where people want to live. That's the kind of market intelligence you will garner in your area as you become more aware of what is going on around you.

Don't assume that everyone has this knowledge, they don't. You can make the most of your expertise in your own backyard by backing your judgement and I am confident when the time comes you will buy the right property. When buying to let, buy the same type of properties where you were inundated with applications from tenants wishing to rent them. That way you know your house will always be full and the rent and the mortgage will be paid.

But before you part with any cash don't forget to have a survey carried out to highlight any deficiencies. That money is always well spent. And when you look at the survey, look at it with open eyes. Don't immediately assume the house is a non-runner. Do your arithmetic again, try to get a discount on the price, don't run away from a deal until you are sure the figures don't add up.

Operate in the areas you know
Check out every property in person
Don't part with money
to people you don't know
Always have a survey done
If it looks too good to be true, it probably is!

Chapter 25: Making Money in Property on a Falling Market

Making money in property during a falling market has traditionally been the hardest thing to achieve. In the past, most property dealers made large profits when prices rose and tended to sit it out and grin and bear it when prices fell.

Today there are real alternatives to losing money in falling markets, so how can you make money in property in a falling market?

When dealers first think they spot a falling market sliding over the horizon towards them, the first port of call would usually be to bale out completely, get rid, full stop. But this can be an expensive business in itself, especially for the smaller operator. For example if you owned a property worth £275,000 and decided that the market was about to fall, and sold, you would need to look very carefully at the arithmetic before you did so. Especially if it was your intention to jump back in as soon as prices flattened out.

If you sold that house, your estate agency fees would be around £4,846 including vat, (based on 1.5%), say £750 for a solicitor, and another £1,000 to move out, assuming you actually lived there in the first place. You're already looking at the thick end of £6,600 in costs, money that has in effect disappeared, and that's not counting any rental expenses you would incur if you went into rented accommodation while you looked around to buy another house.

Regardless of whether the market then moved up, down or sideways, let us assume you then decided to come back into the market six months later and paid the same price

219

for a different home, £275,000. Your likely costs this time are £1,000 to move again, another £750 for your solicitor, a whopping £8,250** in stamp duty, and quite feasibly another £1,000 in mortgage arrangement fees and miscellaneous charges.

Your total costs (or put another way, LOSS) to move in and out, would be around £17,600. In other words when you first imagined the market would fall, it would have to have dropped below £257,400 before you saw any profit from your move. Or put more simply, if you didn't think the market was going to drop by more than £17,600 you would have been better to stay exactly where you were, and saved yourself the hassle and expense that moving inevitably brings.

** Please check the stamp duty calculations on this example, as rates may well have changed since this was written.

THERE ARE OTHER WAYS:

So if you believe the market was in for a fall, the first thing you need to do is estimate how much of a drop. Remember, a small fall almost certainly means you would be better off to stay put. So what else could you do to offset any price damage?

Fortunately in this day and age there are viable easier alternatives and here's one of them, and I'll wager you haven't thought of this. If you think the value of your property is about to fall, but don't want to move, why not have a bet on that fact? A bet? Yes exactly that, a bet!

IGIndex run a variety of house price bets. This is the blurb from their web site to do with house price transactions:

Our average house price bets give you the chance to profit from the housing market without the expense and effort of actually buying (or selling) property.

Spread betting lets you back your judgement on the state of the housing market quickly and with minimal outlay thereby avoiding many of the pitfalls often associated with investing in property. Betting on house prices may sound odd, but it provides a simple and effective way to gain exposure to changes in the market. It also holds certain key advantages over purchasing property directly.

No red tape, expenses or delays.
You can speculate instantly.
No stamp duty or capital gains tax.
All profits are tax-free.
No need to put up the full value.
Go long (buy) or short (sell).
Profit from market volatility.

House price bets are measured against prices reported by the Halifax Bank of Scotland whose report is published monthly. You can obtain further information on the Halifax service on www. hbosplc.com.

Now the first thing that has to be said about that, is that spread betting is an exceedingly risky business. Don't go anywhere near it without fully understanding the market and the procedures involved and particularly, your TOTAL risk.

When you open a spread betting position your risk is NOT limited to the amount of money you have put up, it could run to many times that. If you don't fully understand what you are doing, then DON'T DO IT!

However it does provide a useful tool, especially in a rapidly falling market, whereby you could minimise the fall in the value of your property by hedging in this manner. Of course if you sold short, and the market continued to rise, you would incur a loss, and possibly a big loss. And if you did so, no one would be responsible for that, other than yourself. But that applies to any financial contract you enter into doesn't it? Houses, shares, pensions, endowment policies, it's easy to lose money in all of these if you get it wrong.

Cantor Index and City Index might also be worth checking out to see if they are running similar property price markets too. If you were confident property prices were dropping substantially, but didn't want to sell, you could back your judgement by utilising this method. That's all I'm saying, it's an idea, a suggestion. Please don't think ill of me if the market doesn't do as YOU expect.

VERY IMPORTANT WARNING!!!

Always remember, hedging house prices is a very risky and dangerous business and clearly not for everyone, but I for one would certainly be happy to use these tools if the circumstances warranted it. As they say in stocks and shares DYOR. Do your own research. As they say on Big Brother, You Decide! I am not recommending this course of action, I am simply bringing it to your notice as a possible alternative to minimising the loss involved with falling house prices.

Spread Betting is very dangerous!
Do not put at risk more than you can afford to lose
Make sure you FULLY understand the market and your risk BEFORE becoming involved.

Chapter 26: Your 21 Income Stream Business

As your business grows and prospers you could develop into a 21 income stream business. True, you may decide to pass on certain aspects, but they are all there for you if you decide to incorporate them. To recap, they include:

- Tenants processing fees
- Landlords, who don't want management, one off fee
- Landlords, under management initial fee
- Landlords, monthly management fee
- Insurance premiums commission
- Commission on buy-to-let mortgages
- Renewing tenancy agreements
- Preparing Inventories
- Providing Housing Benefit consultations
- Property Maintenance work for your landlords and others
- Solving landlords and tenants disputes
- Selling space on your property web site to private individuals
- Selling space on your property web site to other agents
- Earning commission through click through banners
- Reducing costs on utility bills
- Recruit agents to sell cheaper utilities paying you commission
- Interest on cash deposits you have collected
- Preparing tenancy agreements for third parties

- Commission on properties that you have sold for others
- Collecting rental on the properties you now own
- Making money on properties you have bought to refurbish and sell on

It's an impressive list, and in any twelve-month period I would expect to earn money in all twenty-one sections. The secret to running a profitable business is to keep your overheads as low as possible, keep your margins as high as you can, and introduce new revenue streams whenever you see them, especially ones that cost little to start, and take up a minimal amount of your time.

When you combine that with keeping your risks low, almost eliminating bad debt, you have a winning formula. Property letting and management is a winning formula and it is no surprise to me that the national groups such as Belvoir, Martin & Co, and Link-Up amongst others have enjoyed great success. You can too, without the need for thousands of pounds of royalty and sign-up fees.

Seek Out New Revenue Streams
Especially ones that Require Little Work
Keep an Open Mind
Keep up with Changing Trends

Chapter 27: Stamp Duty

You might be surprised to learn that Assured Shorthold Tenancy agreements do attract stamp duty, and you'd be in good company if you were. ** See below.

When I informed a landlord that his tenancy agreement attracted stamp duty he told me in no uncertain terms I was talking drivel and plainly did not know what I was talking about. I asked him why he was so certain he was right. He told me he'd been advised by the largest and longest established letting agent in the town that AST's did not attract stamp duty.

I politely told him again he was wrong, and so were they! An hour later the boss of the same lettings company rang me up. She was a middle-aged career woman with a whining voice. "Assured Shortholds are NOT subject to stamp duty", she insisted. I faxed her a copy of the Inland Revenue guide to Stamp Duty relating to AST's. Ten minutes later she rang me back and apologised. Her parting words were " I'm just amazed".

The fact is that most Assured Shorthold Tenancy agreements ARE subject to stamp duty, but equally it is a fact that the vast majority of AST's are never stamped.

Why? Because it is an expense that landlords and tenants can easily avoid, and more often than not, they choose to do so. And because it is so easy to avoid, many landlords, and it has to be said agents too, are not even aware of their responsibilities with regard to stamp duty.

STAMP DUTY IS BASED ON THE TOTAL RENTAL:

The tenancy agreement attracts stamp duty based on the total rental payable and on whether the property is furnished or unfurnished. The completed agreement should be sent off to your local revenue office accompanied by a cheque for the amount payable.

However failure to having your documents stamped does not in itself invalidate agreements. But if legal proceedings were instigated by either the landlord or the tenant to enforce the terms of the agreement in court, the documents may not be used in evidence unless they are stamped.

I have come across cases where the stamp office have refused to stamp an agreement after thirty days from the start of the tenancy, and clearly if that happened it might be difficult to enforce an agreement through the courts if it remained unstamped.

As I said earlier the vast majority of AST's are prepared and run perfectly satisfactorily without ever being stamped, but it is important that you understand that if everything is done absolutely by the book, they should be.

TO STAMP OR NOT:

You have the choice to decide whether to have your agreements stamped or not. And even if you choose not to, you at least know now that the requirement is there. The next time you hear a landlord or an agent spouting off that AST's do not come within the boundaries of stamp duty, you can politely correct them.

So where and when should stamp duty be paid? The first deciding factor is whether the property is furnished or unfurnished. For a property to be described as furnished it should include beds, tables, chairs and cooking facilities. In law there is no such thing as a partly furnished property, it's either furnished or it isn't.

If the property is furnished and the total annual rental is £5,000 or less there is NO stamp duty due. (£416.66 per month, or £96.15 per week.) Neither is there any duty payable if the agreement is for only six months, and the total collected rental does not exceed £5,000. For example the total monthly rental could be as high as £832.32 or a weekly rental of £192.30 for six months. The key point to bear in mind is that the total rental collected should not exceed £5,000 for the period in question. Once the £5,000 figure is scheduled to be exceeded stamp duty is payable as follows.

Stamp Duty is levied on the amount of rental paid at a calculation of 1% per annum and is rounded up in units of £5. The minimum   figure payable is £5. So if the total collectable annual rent were £7,000 the stamp duty would be £70. If the rental were £7,200 the stamp duty would be £75, because it is rounded up to the nearest fiver.

Here's a handy tip that could save you and your clients money.

If the property is let for less than a one-year period, even if the amount of rent collected is scheduled to be more than £5,000, the total stamp duty payable is just £5! Therefore the astute agent and landlord might consider preparing agreements for 364 days, rather than an annual one, especially on higher rental contracts. By doing so it would restrict the stamp duty payable to just £5 and it's perfectly legal.

Stamp duty should be paid within thirty days of the agreement becoming effective. Interest charges can be levied if the stamp duty is paid late.

On unfurnished property on most agreements stamp duty is not dissimilar to furnished agreements, providing the letting period is less than seven years.

I suggest that if you are intending to have your agreements stamped you budget for the same figures as with furnished property. Check with the local revenue stamp office, they will confirm the exact figure for you.

If both the landlord and tenant both sign a separate copy of the agreement one would attract stamp duty at the full rate, and the other at a fixed charge of £5. Before a duplicate can be stamped the stamp office would need proof that an original had previously been stamped at the full rate.

Whether the landlord or the tenant pays the larger of the two rates would be for the agent to negotiate before the tenancy agreement was drawn up.

The addresses where the agreements should be sent are all listed in the directory at the end of this book together with telephone numbers and web site address where you can obtain all the information you need. It's a good idea to speak to the stamp office initially and they will send you a free supply of booklets that you can issue to your clients.

Rather oddly the majority of tenancy agreements prepared in this country today do NOT go to the stamp office for stamping. That is the agents and landlord choice, and the tenancies run through with never a problem. But equally, the vast majority of tenancy agreements in this country today are not being prepared completely by the book.

It is for you to decide. To stamp, or not to stamp, that is the question? Me? I stamped, of course I did. For years and years. Then one day, I stopped, because none of my competitors ever bothered either. It's a small risk you take. I have noticed that many solicitors don't have their agreements stamped either, so what does that say? If a stamp free environment is OK for them, who am I to say differently? Check it out and make up your own mind.

** VERY IMPORTANT UPDATE ON STAMP DUTY:

Since I wrote the above section on Stamp Duty the government has acted to deal with the ridiculous situation where so many agreements were not being correctly stamped. They have now abolished the old arrangements for Stamp Duty on assured shorthold tenancies and have replaced it with the new Stamp Duty Land Tax. (SDLT).

Stamp Duty Land Tax is payable at a rate of 1% of the total rental of the tenancy, but there is NO SDLT payable on residential tenancies, providing the total rental does not exceed £60,000 per annum. As the vast majority of tenancies do not have rental exceeding this figure it has served in effect, to abolish stamp duty on AST's for the huge majority of residential properties, and all property letting agencies will be grateful for that.

But this is a good reminder of how important it is to keep up to date and abreast of all developments within the property industry, and the internet is the easiest and most cost effective way to do this.

Chapter 28:
So that's all there is to it then?

You now know everything there is to know about buying, selling, and renting property in Britain today. Well, sorry, you don't!

You didn't believe that qualified surveyors spend their five years training sitting around playing cards and drinking tea did you? When all they really needed to do was read this book. A likely story.

I liken the property industry to the planet Jupiter. Huge and cloudy, swirling, forever changing, always on the move, magnificent and mysterious. You will NEVER know all there is to know about property, no one ever does, no one ever will, circumstances change, legislation changes. It's up to you to educate yourself and keep abreast of the latest developments.

Joining a trade association is an ideal way to do this as they will send you huge quantities of paperwork, magazines, memos, bulletins, and they will grant you access to member's only sections on their web sites. They are not cheap to join, but are invaluable, and I strongly recommend you join at least one association.

Read everything you can lay your hands on, and study. Learn from your own deals and lettings; learn from your mistakes, for you will surely make some along the way. The best education of all is practical. You will certainly learn far more from your actual transactions, both the successful ones, and the less so, than I or anyone else could ever show you.

But you do now have sufficient knowledge to set about launching you own property letting and management business. And you could do so with only a few hundred pounds seed capital. You have many contacts and sources of information where you can increase your expertise. You have the sources to obtain tenancy agreements and all the other related documentation.

You know where and how you can locate properties, you know how to set about your advertising, you know what to say to landlords and tenants alike, and you know what your target is. To become the BEST letting agent in the town, and that won't be as hard to achieve as you might think. Some of your competitors will be hot, but equally some of your competitors will be will tired and disinterested.

You certainly now know far more than I did when I first started, and if I could then rent, refurbish and sell thousands of properties, then why couldn't you? There's absolutely no reason at all.

Enjoy your business, keep a smile on your face, remain optimistic and determined, provide an efficient, honest and ethical service, forever seek to improve, and you will be successful.

If you are anything like me, you will rush through this book, then toss it to one side, and get started and there is nothing wrong with a sense of urgency, but do make a note to return to these pages every month or so, at least in the early days, and check your progress with that outlined here. In the heat of battle it's so easy to forget a particular aspect of any business, and regular revision always pays dividends.

I would welcome your feedback on any aspect covered in this publication. Your comments may be incorporated in future editions of this work. I'd especially like to hear from you if there is any particular area you would like me to cover in more detail, or indeed if there's any facet I haven't touched upon.

But I regret I'm unable to reply to specific questions on particular property transactions, because they can be so time consuming.

As for me, I am already working on my follow up, SPLAM 2, the sequel! *Coming to a cinema near you!* Look out for it. Thanks for staying through to the end, and good luck in all your property dealings in the future. I wish you well, and great success.

TRADE   DIRECTORY

AFFILIATE MARKETING COMPANIES

www. affiliatemarketing.co.uk
www. affiliatefuel.com
www. cj.com
www. paidonresults.com
www. ukaffiliates.com
www.tradedoubler.com

COMPUTER SOFTWARE SUPPLIERS – PROPERTY SPECIALISTS

CARL
Computer Aided Residential Lettings
84 Beal Lane
Shaw, Lancs OL2 8BH
Tel: 0845 345 5591
Fax: 01706 880800
www. carlcomms.co.uk
Email: info@carlcomms.co.uk
www. rentacomm.net
www. key-data.co.uk
www. professional-property-letting.co.uk
www. fast-data.co.uk
tel: 01634 232464

CREDIT   CHECKING   AND   REFERENCING AGENCIES

Homelet
Tel: 0845 117 6000
Fax: 0845 117 6001

www. homelet.co.uk

Letsure
www. letsure.co.uk

HOUSE PRICE BETTING & HEDGING:

www. igindex.com
www.cityindex.com
www.cantorindex.com

PROFESSIONAL INDEMNITY INSURANCE

Hanover Park Commercial Limited
Phoenix House
Wellesley Road
Croydon CR0 2NW
Tel: 0845 345 0815
Web: www. hanover-park.co.uk

Professional Indemnity insurance may also be
Available through the various trade associations

PROPERTY INSURANCE POLICIES

Homelet
Tel: 0845 117 6000
Fax:0845 117 6001
www. homelet.co.uk

Letsure
www. letsure.co.uk

The NFRL
www. nfrl.org.uk

PROPERTY WEB SITES

www. rightmove.co.uk
www. fish4homes.co.uk
www. ukhomes4sale.co.uk
www. property-renting-online.co.uk
www. homestore.com (USA)
www. lettingzone.com
www. hbosplc.com

REDUCED PRICED UTILITIES

Telecom Plus PLC
www. telecomplus.org.uk/676159

STAMP DUTY OFFICES

Belfast Stamp Office
Ground Floor
Dorchester House
52 – 58 Great Victoria Street
Belfast BT2 7QE
Tel: 028 90 505127

Birmingham Stamp Office
5th Floor, Norfolk House
Smallbrook Queensway
Birmingham B5 4LA
Tel: 0121 633 3313

Bristol Stamp Office
The Pithay
All Saints Street
Bristol BS1 2NY
Tel: 0117 927 2022

Edinburgh Stamp Office
Grayfield House, Spur X
5 Bankhead Avenue
Edinburgh EH11 4AE

Tel: 0131 442 3161

London Stamp Office:
Personal Callers Only to:
South West Wing
Bush House
Strand
London WC2B 4QN
Tel: 0207 438 7252 or 7452

Manchester Stamp Office
Upper 5th floor
Royal Exchange
Exchange Street
Manchester M2 7EB
Tel: 0161 834 8020

Newcastle Stamp Office
4th Floor
Weardale House
Washington
Tyne and Wear NE37 1LW
Tel: 0191 261 1199

Worthing Stamp Office
Postal Applications Only
Room 35, East Block
Barrington Road
Worthing, Sussex
Tel: 01903 508962

Web site address for all stamp duty queries:

www. inlandrevenue.gov.uk/so

SIGN MANUFACTURERS

www. agencyexpress.co.uk

www. estate-signs.co.uk
www. curtisscreenprint.co.uk

STATIONERY SUPPLIERS

Neat Ideas
www. neat-ideas.com
Tel: 01302 890089

Office World
www. office-world.co.uk
Freephone 0800 5000 24

Staples Stationery
www. staples.co.uk
FREE Tel hotline: 0800 6929292

Viking Direct
Freephone: 0800 424444
Fax: 0800 622211
www. viking-direct.co.uk

TRADE ORGANISATIONS & ASSOCIATIONS

ARLA
The Association of Residential Letting Agents
www. arla.co.uk

The Law Society
www. solicitors-online.co.uk

NAEA
The National Association of Estate Agents
www. naea.co.uk

NFRL
The National Federation of Residential Landlords

www. nfrl.org.uk

The Royal Institute of Chartered Surveyors
www. rics.org.uk

TRAINING FOR PROFESSIONALS
Tel: 01258 858585
Email: tfplettingnetwork.com

UKALA
The United Kingdom Association of Letting Agents
www. ukala.org.uk

TRADE PUBLICATIONS

The Estates Gazette
Britain's oldest property magazine founded in 1858
www. estatesgazettegroup.com

The Agreement Magazine
Obtain through the Association of Residential Letting Agents at
www. arla.co.uk

The Estate Agent Magazine
Order through the National Association of Estate Agents at
www. naea.co.uk

Lettings Update
Available through the UK Association of Letting Agents
www. ukala.org.uk

WEB DESIGN SERVICES

www. partnershop.co.uk/shop/1598

Web names registered from just £1.99. Hosting from just £4 per month. Design templates and comprehensive help files.

WEB TRAFFIC GENERATOR PROGRAMS

www. trafficswarm.com/go.cgi?279577
www. freenetleads.com/free/1138car

* Please note that any contact listed here is not necessarily a recommendation. Some of these companies I have never personally used.

At-a-glance Conversion Table.
Weekly Rental To Monthly

Weekly	Monthly:
£50 weekly rental equates to	£216.66
£55	£238.33
£60	£260.00
£65	£281.66
£70	£303.33
£75	£325.00
£80	£346.66
£85	£368.33
£90	£390.00
£95	£411.66
£100	£433.33
£105	£455.00
£110	£476.66
£115	£498.33
£120	£520.00
£125	£541.66
£130	£563.33
£135	£585.00
£140	£606.66
£145	£628.33
£150	£650.00
£155	£671.66
£160	£693.33
£165	£715.00
£170	£736.66
£175	£758.33
£180	£780.00

£185	£801.66
£190	£823.33
£195	£845.00
£200	£866.66
£205	£888.33
£210	£910.00
£215	£931.66
£220	£953.33
£225	£975.00
£230	£996.66
£235	£1018.33

Glossary of Trade Terms and Abbreviations

ARLA: Association of Residential Letting Agents
AST: Assured Shorthold Tenancy
CH: Centrally heated
COMPLETION: The day when transfer of ownership of a property takes place (on purchases and sales)
CONVEYANCING: Legal term for the buying and selling process
COVENANTS: rules and regulations governing the property contained in its title deeds or its lease
CORGI: The Confederation for the Registration of Gas Installers
DG: Double glazed
DILAPIDATION: A claim made against the tenant for damage and excessive wear to a property
DIP: Decision in principle
DISBURSEMENTS: the fees that your solicitor has to pay such as stamp duty, land registration and search fees (on purchases and sales)
DPC: Damp proof course
E & O E: Errors and omissions excepted

EXCHANGE OF CONTRACTS: This is the point at which both the buyer and seller are legally bound by the deal (on purchases and sales)

FF: fully furnished

F&F: Fixtures and fittings

FFF: First floor flat

GCH: Gas central heating

GF: Ground floor

GROUND RENT: The annual charge payable by the leaseholders to the owner of the freehold

FREEHOLD: land and/or buildings held by owner in absolute possession

FRI: Full repairing and insuring lease

HBO: Housing benefit office

IPT: Insurance premium tax

LAND REGISTRATION FEE: Fee paid to verify legal title and rights over a property and to register the ownership of a property with the Land Registry

LEASE: A contract by which land or buildings is conveyed for a specific time by its owner (the lessor) to tenant (the lessee) normally for rent

LEASEHOLDER: A person having tenure over a property by lease

MP: Monthly premium

NAEA: National Association of Estate Agents

NICEIC: National Inspection Council of Electrical Installation Contracting

OA: Offers above

OIEO: Offers in excess of

OIRO: Offers in the region of

O/O: Offers over

OPP: Outline planning permission

PCM: Per calendar month

PF: Partly furnished

POA: Price on application

PI: Professional Indemnity (Insurance)

PP: Planning permission

PTD: Pre tenancy determination, procedure whereby the benefit office will advise what portion of the rental they will pay, prior to the tenant taking up occupation

RICS: Royal Institute of Chartered Surveyors

SCHEDULE: Notification of housing benefit payments, usually 4-weekly

SDLT: Stamp Duty Land Tax, the replacement for traditional Stamp Duty on assured shorthold tenancies.

SOM: Standing Order Mandate

SPLAM: Successful Property Letting And Management

STAMP DUTY: Duty imposed by the government on certain types of legal documents and transactions, such as property deals

STRUCTURAL SURVEY: A full report on the condition of the property, carried out by a qualified surveyor

TENANCY: Period of holding land or property as a tenant

TITLE DEEDS: The documents that show who has the title or right of ownership to a property

UKALA: United Kingdom Association of Letting Agents

UNF: Unfurnished

If you have any comment to make regarding this book, feedback of any kind, ideas and suggestions for any sequels that may be published, I would like to hear from you. You can contact me through my web site:

www.dncarter.co.uk

WEB NAMES FOR SALE:

I have the following property related registered web names
currently for sale, plus one two others too. If you are
interested in any of these, please email your best offer

Worldwidecottages.com
Worldwidecottages.co.uk
Keyagency.co.uk
Blackestates.co.uk
Whiterentals.co.uk
Coastalrentals.co.uk
Greenrentals.co.uk
Riverestates.co.uk
Riverrentals.co.uk
IDCPublishing.co.uk
Blacksports.co.uk
Creditcardgate.co.uk

If interested in any of these please contact me through my
web site www. dncarter.co.uk

Special thanks to all those at lulu.com for all their help in
the production of this book.

I'd also like to thank Anne Sellars for her proof reading
work
and tireless ongoing encouragement

Printed in the United Kingdom
by Lightning Source UK Ltd.
116661UKS00001B/223

9 781411 634442